Small Things Theatre presents

Anything Is Possible If You Think About It Hard Enough

by Cordelia O'Neill

Anything Is Possible If You Think About It Hard Enough premiered at the
Southwark Playhouse, London, on 22 September 2021

.

Cast

ALEX	Gemma Lawrence
RUPERT	Huw Parmenter

Creative Team

Writer	Cordelia O'Neill
Director	Kate Budgen
Designer	Camilla Clarke
Associate Designer	Ceci Calf
Lighting	Sally Ferguson
Sound	Beth Duke
Movement Director	Lucy Cullingford
Producer	Philip Scott-Wallace
Casting	Abby Galvin
Stage Manager	Olivia Boyd
Production Manager	Jack Boissieux

Biographies

Gemma Lawrence – ALEX

Theatre credits as a writer and actor include OFFIE-nominated *Sunnymead Court* (Arcola Theatre/Actor's Centre/UK tour). Her other theatre acting credits include *Not Talking* (Arcola Theatre); *Five Plays: Nuclear* (Young Vic); *Wasted* (Orange Tree Theatre); *All My Sons* (Hong Kong Arts Festival); *The Tempest* (Southwark Playhouse); *As You Like It, Children of the Sun* (National Theatre); *Much Ado About Nothing* (Shakespeare's Globe); *Gaslight* (Salisbury Playhouse); *Lee Harvey Oswald* (Finborough Theatre); *The Cherry Orchard* (Bristol Tobacco Factory, Rose Theatre); and *Rough Cuts: The Lion's Mouth* (Royal Court Theatre). Her television credits include *Shakespeare and Hathaway, 18 – Clash of Futures, Luther, Misfits, 1066, Waking the Dead, Time of Your Life, Stir it Up, All About George, Ahead of the Class* and *Silent Witness*. Her film credits include *Frail, A Bunch of Amateurs* and *Enlightenment*.

Huw Parmenter – RUPERT

Theatre credits include *The Lovely Bones* (Birmingham REP/UK tour); *The Mirror Crack'd* (Wales Millennium Centre, Salisbury Playhouse); *Jam Jars* (Tristan Bates Theatre); *After Orlando* (Theatre Royal Stratford East, VAULT Festival); *The Late Wedding, The Ballad of Lost Dogs, Home Theatre UK* (Theatre Royal Stratford East); *Dark Tourism* (Park Theatre); *Rebel Rebel* (Theatre503); *Living in the City With or Without Sex* (Old Red Lion Theatre); *Pride and Prejudice* (Kenton Theatre); *Basket Case* (UK tour); and *Hearing the Song* (Orange Tree Theatre). Television credits include *Killing Eve, Vikings* and *EastEnders*. Film credits include *Close*.

Cordelia O'Neill – Writer

Cordelia is a writer, actress and co-founder of Small Things Theatre. She trained at Oxford School of Drama. She wrote sell-out show *The Stolen Inches* (Edinburgh 2015). Her production *No Place For A Woman* ran at Theatre503 and has been optioned by Cannibal Films. She is currently writing the screenplay. Her play *The Vote* about women's suffrage with E17 Puppet Theatre Company toured in summer 2018, and finished at HighTide's Walthamstow Festival. She also co-authored *The Apologists* at which premiered at VAULT Festival and was revived at the Omnibus Theatre in Clapham, London.

Kate Budgen – Director

Kate trained at Birkbeck College and on the NT Studio Directors course. She has been a Creative Associate at the Bush Theatre and has worked as Assistant and Associate Director for the Gate Theatre, the Almeida, The Opera Group, Pentabus Theatre, the Bush Theatre, Opera North, and for the Michael Grandage Company. She is an Associate Director on Conor McPherson's *Girl from the North Country*. Selected directing credits include *GUT* (Guildhall School of Music and Drama); *The Importance of Being Earnest* (Watermill Theatre); *Anything Is Possible If You Think About It Hard Enough* (VAULT Festival); *No Place for a Woman* (Theatre503); *Strong Arm* (Underbelly/Old Vic New Voices); *The Hairy Ape* (Southwark Playhouse); *Rigor Mortis* (Papatango/Finborough); *Crossed Keys* (Eastern Angles); *Bedbound* (Lion and Unicorn); *Stoopud Fucken Animals* (Traverse Theatre); *There is a War* (ArtsEd); *Punk Rock* (Guildford School of Acting); *Anne Boleyn* (RWCMD).

Camilla Clarke – Designer

Camilla is a Set and Costume designer based in London, UK. She trained at the Royal Welsh College of Music and Drama, graduating in 2014 with First Class Honours in Theatre Design. Camilla has worked on many projects as an Associate to Designer Chloe Lamford. Productions include *Othello* (Cambridge Arts Theatre, dir. John Haidar); *The Day*

After (ENO Studio Live, dir. Jamie Manton); *The Brief and Frightening Reign of Phil* (New Zealand Festival Theatre, Music and lyrics by Bret McKenzie, dir. Lyndsey Turner); *Inside Bitch* (Royal Court, ass. dir. Milli Bhatia); *Out of Water* (Orange Tree Theatre, dir. Guy Jones); *A Midsummer Night's Dream* (National Youth Theatre, dir. Matt Harrison); *There Are No Beginnings* (Leeds Playhouse, dir. Amy Leach).

Ceci Calf – Associate Designer

Ceci graduated from Royal Welsh College of Music & Drama in 2018, and is now based in London working as both a theatre designer and assistant. Previous design credits include *Rocky Road* (Jermyn Street Theatre); *Not Quite Jerusalem*, *The Wind of Heaven* (Finborough); *One Million Tiny Plays About Britain* (Jermyn Street and Watermill); *Five Green Bottles*, *Tithonus* (Sherman); *Cheer*, *Mydidae* (The Other Room); *The Cut* (LAMDA & Lion and Unicorn); *Yellow Moon* (LAMDA).

Sally Ferguson – Lighting Designer

Lighting credits include *Two* (New Vic Theatre); *Pippi Longstocking* (Royal & Derngate Northampton); *The Last King of Scotland* (Sheffield Crucible); *The Importance of Being Earnest* (Watermill Theatre); *Strange Fruit*, *An Adventure* (Bush Theatre); *Snow White* (Wrong Crowd); *End of the Pier*, *Honour*, *Building the Wall* (Park Theatre); *Carmen the Gypsy* (Arcola Theatre); *To See the Invisible* (Aldeburgh Festival); *Again* (Trafalgar Studios); *Richard III* (Perth Theatre); *31 Hours* (Bunker Theatre); *Aladdin*, *Shiver*, *Lost in Yonkers* (Watford Palace Theatre); *Educating Rita* (Queen's Theatre Hornchurch); *While We're Here* (Farnham Maltings); *Jess And Joe Forever* (Orange Tree Theatre); *The Two Boroughs Project* (Young Vic); *Sweet Charity* (Manchester Royal Exchange); *We Wait in Joyful Hope, And Then Come the Nightjars, Many Moons* (Theatre503); *The Sleeping Beauties* (Sherman Cymru); *As You Like It*, *Floyd Collins* (Southwark Playhouse); *HAG*,

The Girl with the Iron Claws (Wrong Crowd/Soho Theatre); *Microcosm* (Soho Theatre); *Slowly* (Riverside Studios); *Così fan tutte* (Village Underground); *The Marriage of Figaro* (Wilton's Music Hall); *The Wonder! A Woman Keeps a Secret* (BAC).

Beth Duke – Sound Designer

Beth Duke is a theatre sound designer and composer. She was resident sound designer at the Almeida Theatre and recently nominated by the Evening Standard and TikTok as one of the top-six audio designers. Credits include *J'Ouvert* (Harold Pinter Theatre and BBC); *One Jewish Boy* (Trafalgar Studios, West End and UK tour); *Typical Girls* (Sheffield Crucible Theatre); *Scenes with Girls*, *Living Newspaper* (Royal Court Theatre); *Death Drop*, *Tuck Shop West End* (Garrick Theatre); *Patricia Gets Ready* (Pleasance Theatre); *Gentlemen*, *Pipeline*, *A Fantastic Bohemian*, *Lovesick* (Arcola Theatre); *Reimagining* (Almeida Theatre); *Last Easter* (Orange Tree Theatre); *One Under* (Graeae Theatre Company at Plymouth Drum and UK tour); *Superstar*, *Anything Is Possible If You Think About It Hard Enough* (Southwark Playhouse); *New Views* (National Theatre); *Silence* (Mercury Theatre/UK tour); *Instructions for a Teenage Armageddon* (Old Red Lion); *Split!*, *Boots*, *Lovely & Jason*, *Alice*, *Patricia Gets Ready*, *Head of State*, *Goodbear* (VAULT Festival); *Together*, *Not the Same* (Sadler's Wells); *Queen Margaret*, *5/11*, *Emilia* (Mountview); *Great Expectations* (Geffrey Museum); *Around the Block* (Etcetera); *Eros* (White Bear); *Boxman* (UK tour); *Little Did I Know* (Bread & Roses); *The State of Things* (Brockley Jack Studio); *Hamlet* (Royal Central School of Speech and Drama); *Ulsta Americans*, *Hyenas* (LAMDA). Credits as associate include *War of the Worlds Immersive Experience* (56 Leadenhall Street); *A Midsummer Night's Dream* (Tobacco Factory); *Apollo 13* (Original Theatre Company); *Dust* (New York Theatre Workshop).

Lucy Cullingford – Movement Director

Lucy is a Movement Director and Choreographer for Theatre, Opera and dance. She trained at the Northern School of Contemporary Dance and holds an MA in Movement Studies from The Royal Central School of Speech and Drama. Theatre credits include *Death of England*, *All of Us* (National Theatre); *The Wizard of Oz* (Leeds Playhouse). *King Lear* (Minerva Theatre Chichester and West End); *Constellations* (Royal Court/West End/UK tour and Broadway; Donmar Warehouse in the West End). For the Royal Shakespeare Company, credits include *The Taming of the Shrew*, *Measure for Measure*, *Coriolanus*, *The Jew of Malta*, *Snow in Midsummer*, *The Tempest* (motion capture production), *Don Quixote* (RSC and West End).

Abby Galvin – Casting

Associate/Assistant credits for Jessica Ronane Casting for theatre include *4000 Miles*, *Endgame*, *Lungs*, *Present Laughter*, *SYLVIA*, *A Monster Calls* (Old Vic and UK tour), *Mood Music*, *Fanny & Alexander*, *The Divide*, *A Christmas Carol*, *Girl from the North Country* (Old Vic and Toronto/West End), *Woyzeck*, *Rosencrantz & Guildenstern are Dead*, *King Lear*, *The Caretaker*, *The Master Builder*, *Dr. Seuss's The Lorax*, *The Hairy Ape*, *Future Conditional* (Old Vic); *Running Wild* (Regent's Park Open Air Theatre); *Love in Idleness* (Menier Chocolate Factory). Child casting: *School of Rock*, *Charlie and the Chocolate Factory* (West End); *Billy Elliot the Musical*, *Matilda the Musical* (both West End/UK tour); *Bugsy Malone* (Lyric Hammersmith). Casting for film includes *Night Out* (short).

Philip Scott-Wallace – Producer

Phil trained as an actor at LAMDA and is a co-founder of Small Things Theatre. Since the company's formation in 2015, Phil has produced six plays: *The Stolen Inches*, *No Place for a Woman*, *A Gym Thing*, *Leaves*, *Boots* and *Anything Is Possible If You Think About It Hard Enough*. He has also produced seven *Night of Small Things*, the theatre company's variety night showcasing the best in music, theatre, comedy and poetry that the capital has to offer. In addition to this Phil pioneered a collaboration between UN Women and the VAULT Festival in 2018 for their HeForShe ArtsWeek. This included a special *Night of Small Things* including work from Tony Award winner Simon Stephens and West End playwright Tamsin Oglesby. Alongside this he curated an evening on gender equality with a discussion featuring BAFTA winner and writer Robert Webb, Chi Onwurah MP, Sophie Walker leader of Women's Equality Party, Matthew Ryder Deputy Mayor of London and David Brockway of the Great Men Initiative.

Olivia Boyd – Stage Manager

Olivia trained at the Royal Central School of Speech and Drama, completing a BA (Hons) degree in Stage Management. Her theatre credits include *Shedding a Skin* (Elayce Ismail, Soho Theatre); *A Midsummer Night's Dream* (Turbine Theatre and Buxton Opera House); *Uncle Vanya* (Harold Pinter, Sonia Friedman Productions and All3Media); *Dr Faustus* (Cockpit Theatre); *FriendsFestive* (Comedy Central and Luna Cinema); *Urinetown: The Musical* (Chelsea Walker, Embassy Theatre); *Welcome to Thebes* (Oliver Dimmesdale and Ferdy Roberts of Filter Theatre) and *Anatomy of a Suicide* (Irina Brown, Webber Douglas Studio).

SMALL THINGS THEATRE brings detailed, entertaining, and socially thought-provoking work to the stage. They produce new plays, provide a platform for new artists in theatre, music, comedy and poetry, and have curated work to raise money for Grenfell survivors and the UN Women's gender equality campaign.

They have collaborated with the Pleasance, Theatre503, The Vaults and now Southwark Playhouse to produce new work from Cordelia O'Neill, Tom Vallen and Jess Butcher. They were also commissioned by UN Women and Vaults to curate a special performance of new work supporting HeForShe arts week, with a worldwide call out for short plays to accompany new work from writers Simon Stephens and Tamsin Oglesby on theme of gender equality. Alongside, they hosted a discussion with Robert Webb, leading politicians and charities about what actually helps redress the balance between genders.

Past productions include *No Place for a Woman* (Theatre503), *A Gym Thing* (Pleasance Theatre, Edinburgh and London), *Leaves* (Caravanserail Bookshop), and *The Stolen Inches* (Edinburgh Festival Fringe).

Twitter: @smallthingstc
Facebook: @smallthingstheatre
Instagram: @smallthingstheatre
www.smallthingstheatre.com
#AnythingIsPossiblePlay

Acknowledgements

We are hugely grateful to everyone who has helped realise this play.
Some of those who have been extremely generous with their time and
allowed us a window into their world are:

Fiona & Niall Cassidy, parents of Matilda.
Karen Burgess, founder of Petals the bereavement counselling charity.
Alyx Elliott, mother of Skye.
Jane Scott, senior bereavement midwife at St Mary's Hosptial
Paddington
Lauren Hutton, senior bereavement midwife at St Mary's Hosptial
Paddington
Sam Doré, midwife at UCL Hospital.
David Monteith, father of Grace and founder of Grace In Action.
Jen Coates and Jennifer Reed from SANDS the stillbirth and neonatal
death charity.
Jen Reid from Teddy's Wish.
Professor Alexander Heazell from Tommy's Rainbow Clinic,
Manchester.
Emma Tomlinson Lead Midwife at Tommy's Rainbow Clinic,
Manchester.
Illona Linthwaite, mother of Eliza.
Rupal Pert, mother of Aryan.

We'd also like to thank Taz Martin for rehearsal and production shots
(@tazmartinphoto / info@tazmartinphotography.com); Lizzie Gilson
for filming our interviews; Kate Morley, Hannah Margerison and
Georgie Grant from Kate Morley PR; George Wallace and all those
who contributed to our fundraising for the show; Milo McGrath for
our set build; Raffaela Pancucci for stepping in to help with sound;
Father Brian at St Barnabas Bethnal Green for a beautiful rehearsal
space; Chris, Susie, Corinne, Charlotte, Cat, Lee and the rest of the
Southwark Playhouse team; and finally our dear friend Holly Wilding
whose experience inspired the story.

We dedicate the play to all the babies who live in the stars.

How We Remember Edward

When we fell pregnant with our first baby Edward, we were overjoyed and so excited to be parents for the first time.

After a long and complicated labour, our big healthy baby boy arrived on 18th January 2014. We could never have imagined what the joy and love of becoming parents would feel like. Eddie was perfect and finally our family was complete.

But that all changed in the early hours of April 16th. Just three short months later, we tragically and unexpectedly lost Edward when he was only three months old to SIDS (sudden infant death syndrome), formerly known as cot death. In that moment, our whole life was irrevocably shattered.

On every medical test possible, Edward was perfectly healthy. We were left with no reason or attributable cause as to why our baby boy left us. The unknown and the unanswered questions made our grief so much harder to bear.

Losing a child is every parent's worst nightmare. No parent should ever outlive their child. It flows completely against the natural order of life and is the worst loss imaginable. As a parent you are meant to protect your child. We felt helpless and that we had failed Edward and failed as parents.

To further complicate our grief, Edward was our first and only child. Losing Edward, our whole identity changed. Everything became past tense. We were parents. We were a family. We had a baby boy. Now it was just the two of us. Chris and Jen. How could we continue to be parents when Eddie wasn't here? We were bereft and broken.

When we said goodbye to Edward at the hospital, Chris and I made a promise. We would live our lives for Edward and make him proud in everything we do. Just three months later, we set up a charity to search for answers and to honour Edward's memory. We know that SIDS is just one form of baby loss and we firmly believe that no parent should ever suffer the loss of a child. For those that do, support is so critical in giving those families hope to live their life's again. Our charity, Teddy's Wish, funds potentially life-saving research into the causes of SIDS, neonatal death and stillbirth, and provides bereavement support for grieving families. Crucially, the charity allows us to continue to parent Edward in some way.

Whilst we know the charity won't bring our baby boy back, our hope is that it will help others and that will be a fitting way to honour Edward's memory and make him proud of his mummy and daddy.

Jen Reid
Teddy's Wish

Fiona and Niall Cassidy

On the 6th October 2016, Niall and I left our flat expecting we would meet our first baby very soon. As parents to be we knew our lives were about to change but little did we know how it would turn out and change us forever.

After trying to find a heartbeat we heard the words 'I'm sorry there is nothing we can do.' With support and care from our amazing midwives we made it through the delivery and our baby girl, Matilda, was born still on the 7th October 2016. At forty-one weeks and three days she was supposed to come out screaming but there was only silence. It's a life-changing moment that I hope no one else ever has to go through but sadly as we soon came to realise that's not the case.

The hospital supported us through those first few days. Helping us to create as many memories with her as possible. Our immediate family came and had a chance to hold and see Matilda. I still treasure those days we had with her so much. The memory box the team prepared for us was amazing and it's certainly a very prized possession. To have her tiny footprints keeps her memory alive.

As time passes and life seems to continue around us, we managed to pick ourselves up. The first Christmas, Mother's Day and Father's Day are all full of emotions and feelings of loss. Sometimes it hurts so bad it's like we're back in that room again hearing the words. Family and friends carried us through the hard days. We were focused on survival and keeping Matilda's memory alive.

Finding out I was pregnant again in March 2017 was exciting, but sadly pregnancy (and parenting) after loss is never the same. You know what can happen and take each day as it comes. I was watched closely and, following some changes in the scan results, our consultant made the decision the time was right to deliver our baby. Not sure if fate or not but Emmeline arrived exactly one year later, sharing her big sister's birthday of 7th October. It was another life-changing day for us, our families and our amazing friends, who have been so supportive.

David and Siobhan Montieth

Memory is a strange thing. It's hard as nails and as whimsical as as the translucence of a butterfly's wings. I remember my daughter's womb life. The time we spent with her without knowing what she looked like, other than a grainy scan which showed she had my nose. I remember the anticipation of my wife's early contractions. I remember the trembling inside when the midwife took longer than normal to find a heartbeat. I remember the blind, vain hope as we drove to the hospital to be scanned.

I remember the world breaking with the words 'I'm sorry' and the inhuman noise from my wife that bookmarked the ending of our old lives and the beginning of our new lives.

I don't remember meeting with the consultants to discuss our choices.

I do remember the birth, a water birth, the best possible birth in the worst possible situation.

I remember my daughter's warmth against my chest as we did skin-to-skin that made me think I was the victim of a cosmic prank and that she actually lived; that caused me to beg her to open her eyes and breathe; to sing 'Beautiful Dreamer' to her.

I remember her weight in my arms which causes me to be too aware of how empty they are when I think her name. I remember her face and fingers and toes, but how can a memory be so vivid and yet feel like it's obscured by a heat haze. I never saw her eyes, I don't remember them.

I have forgotten much of the following two weeks, it is a sporadic series of real-life vignettes, but I do remember the funeral and the love of those that sang 'Amazing Grace' with us.

I remember walking away from the graveside trying to understand how any of this was possible, how I had just watched my daughter, my actual real child, being lowered into the ground, into a hole that I had dug with my own sweat and tears.

I remember things that haven't happened – her first steps, her first words, her first day of school, and so much more. But they are memories more ephemeral than the breeze of a butterfly's wings as they fly past your face because they are memories of the mind's eye, imagination's children.

My memories mess with me, they make me cry, sometimes sob like a baby; they make me ache, they make me smile, they make me proud of both my daughter and my warrior wife and my courageous children.

And then there are the things I don't have to remember, the present day. You see my relationship with my dead daughter is ever-evolving, ever-changing, and with that she affects the way I live almost as much as my living daughters do. She makes me over, her legacy is larger than she was and larger than me. She was real, she changed the world like even the smallest creature can. She was brief but she is eternal.

She is Grace in Action
yeah remember that!

To Eliza

Eliza died before she was born.

I hope Dear Eliza that you are happy for me to write this.

In 1972 I became pregnant. It was not the easiest pregnancy. I was very sick and never seemed to be quite the size I should be. I had a recurring dream in which a small girl was drowning in a basin of water. At the time I dismissed this as natural enough.

The child was due in early July. By May my lack of size was causing some concern but the baby was extremely lively and none of the tests gave cause for any disquiet. However, it was decided that I should have hospital rest and give the doctors time for observation. On the very day that I left some two weeks later, I felt that the baby had become much quieter. Sleep, I thought, he/she is resting. I think I went into denial; a week later I was back in hospital; they told me she had died. It was decided that it would be better for me physically and psychologically to have a natural birth; not to be induced. I should go home and wait. My husband Peter and I did that. We waited.

That summer was magnificent. Late May, early June; a time of explosive natural beauty. We waited and on 7th June before dawn I went into labour. I had a fierce feeling for this child. I wanted to register everything that happened that day and if possible, understand it. I did not want to be knocked out.

The following night was lonely and towards the dawn of 8th June Eliza was born and whisked away. I asked to see her. Better not to, was the reply. The next few days were a whirl of visitors. My husband, mother, brother and friends. But I could only think of Eliza somewhere else, apart and alone. I repeatedly asked to see her. During this time my breasts started producing a huge supply of milk. You would think the body might know but it doesn't. An irony.

One particularly sweet nurse said she understood my need to see Eliza; that she would help to bring this about and be with me. And so it happened. And suddenly I was terrified; had I given birth to some strange being? We were driven to a chapel of rest. It was another brilliant morning. We walked out of the dazzle of the day into a cool white space. A tiny mite lay on a vast bier covered in purple cloth. Eliza – I recognised you. I gave you greeting; you were still and at peace. And I knew then that one day, I would be too.

Peter didn't come with me. He felt it was my need not his. His grief was a different thing. It wasn't the custom then for parents to see a stillborn child. Luckily now it is realised that this is a vital part of recovery. For myself I am certain that, had I not met and acknowledged Eliza as I did, I might not have conceived and given birth to a beautiful son the following year – Jack.

Illona Linthwaite
February 2020

Rupal Pert

My son Aryan was stillborn on 25th January 2018 at 24 weeks +2. His birth, whilst being the one of the most difficult things I've ever had to go through (saying goodbye to him was far harder), was beautiful. It's hard to put into words how heavy the loss of a child is, particularly a loss that others would rather pretend never happened. In the weeks after Aryan was born, I could not imagine how I would ever live and laugh again, but I am here, on the other side, bruised and surprised to have made it through.

I began an Instagram account called sparkjoyinthedark. Why? A week after Aryan was born, my husband and I went shopping to buy a toy for him to have in his coffin. It was a terrible day, but when we stopped and had a coffee, the sun was shining on us and I looked at Dan and felt a lightness in my heart – a spark of joy at how much we loved each other and how beautiful the sunshine was. That was when I decided that I would seek and recognise any spark of joy that came my way to honour Aryan, and photograph it to record it. I choose to seek joy in the darkness of my life after losing him. There are a few days when it's incredibly hard, and there are no sparks of joy at all. Most days however, there is something. Grief weighs my heart down so heavily that I recognise a spark of joy by feeling a lightness in my heart that was not there a second ago. It can last minutes or a split second, but is always a welcome relief from the weight of staring into the abyss. In the first year, I would often get to the end of the day, and look back, thinking it was terrible, heavy and endless – but then I would check my photos and remember there was a spark of joy in my day after all. Now, I find it easier to seek joy, and accept it on a daily basis. Anything can spark joy – from a note left for me to a beautiful meal, from shower curtains to a meme, from graffiti aubergines to a kiss from my daughter.

Finding joy means I can override the grief and sadness, and keep going. I've been told I need to move on, but how does one move on from their child? We have accepted now that life goes on, and that we must move with it. But Aryan moves with us, we remember him in all we do, and we honour him in our living. How do I remember Aryan? I remember him as being the most perfect little boy, with his big sister's eyes, his daddy's ears and his mummy's nose. I remember the love I felt for him during my eventful pregnancy. I remember his tiny fingers and tiny toes. I remember the weight of the silence when he was born, and the shape of the fear of meeting him. I remember him every hour of every day of every month of every year. I remember my son, because although he was stillborn, he was *still born*, and he was born my son.

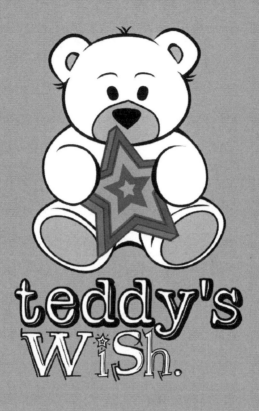

Funding research into
the causes of baby loss.

Providing hope
for grieving families.

www.teddyswish.org

Sands
Stillbirth & neonatal death charity

Our vision is for a world where fewer babies die and when a baby does die, anyone affected receives the best possible care and support for as long as it is needed.

Funding research to save babies' lives

Helping anyone affected by the death of a baby

Working to improve bereavement care

To make a single donation
Text 'SANDS'
and your chosen amount to
💰 **70085**

To make a regular donation
Text 'SANDSREG'
and your chosen amount to
💰 **70085**

If you need support:

📞 Freephone Helpline: 0808 164 3332
🎧 helpline@sands.org.uk
👥 sands.community
🌐 sands.org.uk/support
📱 Sands Bereavement Support App
📖 sands.org.uk/book

General Enquiries:

📞 020 7436 7940
🎧 info@sands.org.uk
🌐 sands.org.uk
💰 **sands.org.uk/donate**

Sands relies almost entirely on voluntary income
and receives very little government funding.

All donations and funds raised by our amazing supporters will go
towards vital services that we offer and activities that meet our core aims.

The difference
we made;

517
bereaved parents and
families helped per month

2,084
memory boxes
provided to parents

2,640
healthcare
professionals trained

*from 2017-2018

The Baby Loss Counselling Charity

Petals is the Baby Loss Counselling Charity.

We provide free-of-charge specialist counselling to support the mental health of individuals and couples who experience pregnancy or baby loss. Our counsellors provide a safe space to guide parents through the grief and trauma of their experience to a place of hope for the future.

www.petalscharity.org

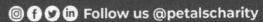 Follow us @petalscharity

Registered Charity No. 1150375

Was it my fault?

1 4 pregnancies end in loss
nd most parents never
d out why.

think that's unacceptable.

#TellMeWHY

ommy's
gether, for every baby

With more research,
we can find the answers
tommys.org/why

Tommy's is registered charity no 1040008 and 3C0(9080)

ANYTHING IS POSSIBLE
IF YOU THINK ABOUT IT HARD ENOUGH

Cordelia O'Neill

Characters

RUPERT
ALEX

A forward slash (/) in the text indicates the point at which the next speaker interrupts.

A lack of punctuation at the end of a line indicates an unfinished thought or the next line following immediately on.

This text went to press before the end of rehearsals and so may differ slightly from the play as performed.

Scene One

RUPERT. A crisp morning, a seat on the Tube, no queues on the
escalator, an easy stroll in the navy suit with the red tie from my
school days that I should have forgotten but I kept to remind me
of success. Shoes polished like my grandfather's and an umbrella
tucked neatly under my arm just in case. I'm smart, I'm a

ALEX *appears and* RUPERT *accidentally hits her with his*
umbrella, hard. It hurts her, but he doesn't notice, until she
shouts.

ALEX. Twat

RUPERT *turns around, watches her walk away. A moment. He*
has lost his train of thought...

RUPERT. I'm a... a...
Green skirt ironed in a rush with straighteners, pink and
yellow jumper clashing, but in a charming way. High-heel
shoes rubbing already. I don't know why she wears them. It's
okay though, there are some grey trainers discarded under her
desk. Hair... a mess. No umbrella despite the weather forecast,
handbag that doesn't quite fit everything, a toothpaste stain
down the clashing jumper, that smile...

Beat.

I work in finance, you already know that... Numbers bore
everyone so I won't bore you.

Beat.

Well. Maybe... Are you interested?

Beat.

You see, for me, I find that you can't not think of numbers, you
can't avoid numbers, day to day numbers are everywhere. That
day for instance, the first day... Alarm at 6:45, snooze for five
minutes, shower in ten, brush teeth for three, dress in seven,
coffee and breakfast for twelve minutes, then three minutes to

put on coat, shoes, collect bag, check the clouds and grab the umbrella. A ten-minute walk to the station, a fourteen-minute train followed by a stupidly long nine-minute change from platform one to four, another six minutes on the train, then if you're smart and know the secret exit a five-minute walk out of the station followed by a seven-point-five-minute walk to the office. Don't judge me for remembering all of that. Don't judge me for enjoying telling you. Don't judge me for loving each individual number. Those numbers are magic, imagine if I had been a minute late? If I snoozed my alarm two minutes too long, my train had been delayed or I had left the umbrella and then had to run back home, pick it up and get on another train, imagine if those numbers had been different well, then none of this...

*

RUPERT. Hello

ALEX (*looking around, bewildered*). Hello?

RUPERT. Hello

ALEX. Hello.

RUPERT. It's me. Umbrella man. I hit you with my umbrella.

ALEX. It's you.

RUPERT. How are you?

ALEX. It's early

RUPERT. It's 8:15

ALEX. It's early.

RUPERT. Coffee?

ALEX. Now?

RUPERT. Yes.

ALEX. We're on the train

RUPERT. I magicked a Thermos of coffee from my goatskin briefcase.

ALEX. Of course

RUPERT. What?

ALEX. Of course you have a Thermos.

RUPERT. She drank my coffee, took a big gulp, said it was

ALEX. Too weak

RUPERT. Then got off.

Scene Two

RUPERT. A Tube strike.
  On a Monday.
  A two-day hangover.
  Drizzle.
  A forgotten Thermos.
  No umbrella.
  Calls for one thing.
  Americano and that almond croissant please.

  RUPERT *turns and runs into* ALEX, *the coffee goes all over
  her, her own coffee drops to the floor, she is soaked, she is
  furious.*

ALEX. Fuck

RUPERT. Oops, / so sorry

ALEX. Fuck it, no, leave it.

RUPERT. It's okay, here let me

ALEX. No, just leave it.

RUPERT. Let me, no, let me buy you a fresh one

ALEX. No, no I don't want one.

RUPERT. Is okay, wait a sec. I'll just nip up / to the...

ALEX. It's you

RUPERT. Oh hello

ALEX. Umbrella man

RUPERT. It's me.

ALEX. Nip up.

RUPERT. Excuse me?

ALEX. You said you'd 'nip up' to the…

RUPERT. Counter

ALEX. I know. 'Nip up.'

RUPERT. It's just another way of saying / go up

ALEX. I know what it means.

RUPERT. Oh
    My mum says it.

ALEX. Your mum? Sweet.

    Beat.

    I didn't take you as an almond-croissant kind of man

RUPERT. Oh you know Monday blues

ALEX. And where is your Thermos?

RUPERT. I forgot it

ALEX. Oh dear

RUPERT. What did you take me for?

ALEX. What?

RUPERT. If not an almond croissant then what?

ALEX. An egg-white-omelette kind of man.

RUPERT. Oh

ALEX. Am I right?

RUPERT. I guess

ALEX. You guess?

RUPERT. I am

ALEX. Thought so.

RUPERT. What do you have for breakfast?

ALEX. Guess

RUPERT. I'm awful at guessing

ALEX. Just guess

RUPERT. No I can't

ALEX. Try

RUPERT. Ummm... Coffee...

ALEX. Nope.

RUPERT. What then?

ALEX. Jam.

RUPERT. Just jam?

ALEX. Yup.

RUPERT. Out of a jar?

ALEX. Exactly

RUPERT. Like a yogurt?

ALEX. Perfect

RUPERT. Do you eat the whole jar?

ALEX. No, I eat just the right amount.

RUPERT. What's the right amount?

ALEX. It depends how I'm feeling

RUPERT. How much did you eat today?

ALEX. A huge amount of raspberry jam.

RUPERT. What's your name?

ALEX. Alex

RUPERT. Jammy Alex.

ALEX. What's yours?

RUPERT. Rupert

ALEX. Like the bear.

*

RUPERT. I began to imagine, began to create pictures. A man, a
crisp white shirt, sleeves folded, breakfast, a place mat, a
napkin, a cafetière, a paper waiting.
A woman, standing in a kitchen, fully dressed but hair in a
towel, odd socks, running late for something but in no rush
and just scrolling through her phone absentmindedly eating a
pot of raspberry Tiptree.

He stops. He smiles. He is remembering.

I can see it.
Shirt, coffee, paper, her. Her towel, her phone, her jam. Her.
She steals my breakfast, I tap her on her nose. She finishes my
coffee, I pull her towel off. This scene, this scene of... Playing
over and over and over, reforming my brain, reshaping my
thoughts changing me in that hour, that minute, that second.
No numbers, timings, schedules just me and her.
I stood and stared at Alex, at Jammy Alex covered in coffee.

*

RUPERT. Wine?

ALEX. Now?

RUPERT. Thursday?

ALEX. A date?

RUPERT. I'd like that.

ALEX. Okay.

RUPERT. Okay, yes?

ALEX. Okay yes, Rupert the Bear.

Scene Three

RUPERT. She was late, forty-five minutes late, blamed it on a
delayed train and rush hour, which was odd as we worked in
the same area. So I spent some time looking at the wine menu,
I love a wine menu. There is something about the pop of the

cork, the glug of wine into the clear glass, the sound, the sniff, the texture. Hints of raspberry, of earth, a little smokiness, a little soil and the slight scent of…

ALEX. Toothpaste

RUPERT. I'm sorry

ALEX. Apple juice and toothpaste, that's what I think of when I drink it.

RUPERT. Oh even with red wine?

ALEX. No, I don't mind red wine, I don't mind white wine. I don't mind wine, I just don't get the buzz, I don't get the long sniffs and aroma chat, I'm like, just drink it, soon it won't matter what it tastes like.

RUPERT. Do you want me to order something else?

ALEX. No wine is fine

RUPERT. I can get bubbles

ALEX. Okay

RUPERT. Do you want bubbles?

ALEX. Yes

RUPERT. Or we can just stick with the Chablis

ALEX. Fine

RUPERT. What would you prefer?

ALEX. I honestly don't mind

RUPERT. Or we could just not drink.

ALEX. God no, it's a first date we need it.

RUPERT. Great, so stick with the Chablis

ALEX. Perfect

RUPERT. We could just do the glass, if you don't really like wine.

ALEX. No a bottle, we need a bottle.

RUPERT. One each?

ALEX. Perfect

RUPERT. I was joking

ALEX. I wasn't

RUPERT. Are you planning on getting really drunk

ALEX. Yes, aren't you?

RUPERT. I thought we could just enjoy the wine?

ALEX. God no, don't you think it's better we just get smashed.

RUPERT. Oh right...

ALEX. First dates, fucking awful if you ask me. Fag?

As she speaks she takes some cigarettes out of her bag and offers RUPERT *one, he declines and then tries his best to listen and stop her from lighting up. She doesn't notice.*

So go on,

RUPERT. Sorry

ALEX. Go on... woo me...

RUPERT. I don't really know how / to woo

ALEX. Tell me what you're like in bed, how your parents fucked you up. Do you like going down on women?

RUPERT. I'm not sure / that's what I would call wooing

ALEX. And don't just say you do because you think I want to hear it, be honest, think about it. Let's reveal it all now. Let's promise to do that okay? Promise? Not three months down the line when we discover our stars aren't aligned, that you snore, pick your nose, wear socks in the bed...

Pause.

RUPERT. Sorry can you?...

ALEX. Slow down? Sorry / I talk at a million miles don't I?

RUPERT. No, it's / just sorry, you can't smoke...

ALEX. I'm relentless. / Sometimes I wonder if I've even breathed

RUPERT. It's fine, / we're outside but it's...

ALEX (*still smoking*). I try and be mysterious and cool,
sometimes I am

RUPERT. It's just / okay. Dammit. Okay they're looking at us.

ALEX. Why?

RUPERT. You're smoking.

ALEX. Did you want one?

RUPERT. Okay, the waiter, is. They're coming over. Right.
Fiddlesticks.

He snatches the cigarette from ALEX*'s hand. And stubs it out.
Panicked. He then waves an apology to the waiters and other
customers.*

Pause.

ALEX. Fiddlesticks?

RUPERT. It's a non-smoking area.

ALEX. We're outside

RUPERT. In the non-smoking area.

*RUPERT takes a big gulp of his drink. He's visibly stressed,
uncomfortable, embarrassed, the whole lot.*

ALEX (*smirking*). You okay matey?

RUPERT. I think so.

He breathes slowly.

I used to be quite asthmatic.

ALEX. Did you?

RUPERT. Used to be quite bad

ALEX. Better now?

RUPERT. Think so

ALEX. Fiddlesticks.

RUPERT. Fiddlesticks

ALEX. Cute

RUPERT. My / mum says it.

ALEX. Does your mum say it?

RUPERT. Yes

ALEX. Do you always do what your mum does?

RUPERT. Yes, all good boys do.

ALEX. HA!

RUPERT. You're a smoker

ALEX. Not really.

RUPERT. Not really?

ALEX. When I'm nervous

RUPERT. You're nervous?

ALEX. Aren't you?

Pause.

RUPERT. You shouldn't smoke

ALEX. I do what I want

She goes to light another cigarette.

RUPERT. Are you serious?

ALEX. No. I'm messing.

RUPERT. We're going to need more wine

ALEX. More wine?

RUPERT. I'm going to have to get very drunk.

ALEX. More wine?

RUPERT. Yes

ALEX. You're not leaving

RUPERT. No.

Pause.

ALEX. This is good, I like this a lot.

RUPERT. You do?

ALEX. Would your mum approve?

RUPERT. No.

ALEX. Ha

RUPERT. She'd be furious

ALEX. Fantastic

RUPERT. She'd be outraged

ALEX. How about your dad? Cigar-smoking, tweed-wearing cricket fan?

RUPERT. I don't have a dad

ALEX. Oh

RUPERT. Just my mum.

ALEX. Did your dad die?

RUPERT. Oh. Ha. Forward. Yes he did.

ALEX. How?

RUPERT. I don't know

ALEX. Why?

RUPERT. I never asked

ALEX. Doesn't your mum talk about him?

RUPERT. She didn't know him.

ALEX. One-night stand?

RUPERT. Um no

ALEX. She was raped?

RUPERT. Jesus no. No. No. Not at all. That's horrid

ALEX. How come she doesn't know him

RUPERT. I'm adopted. She adopted me.

ALEX. Oh

RUPERT. Jesus, why did you say that?

ALEX. Why not?

RUPERT. Why does your mind go there?

ALEX. Where?

RUPERT. To the worst thing? Like the worst possible thing

ALEX. But it is possible

RUPERT. It's not

ALEX. Of course it's possible, anything is.

RUPERT. You're very /

ALEX. Forward

RUPERT. Rude

ALEX. Rude?

RUPERT. Yes.

ALEX. Wow.

RUPERT. Sorry. I don't mean to be

ALEX. Rude

RUPERT. People don't talk like this

ALEX. I'm not most people

Beat.

God that was corny.

RUPERT. That was odd

ALEX. That was gross

RUPERT. That was very unsettling.

ALEX. I'm sorry

RUPERT. You should be

ALEX. From now on I'll only be rude.

RUPERT. Thank you

Pause.

ALEX. So you're the adopted child of a single woman.

RUPERT. Yes

ALEX. Brothers? Sisters?

RUPERT. Just me

ALEX. Interesting

RUPERT. Not really

ALEX. From

RUPERT. Hampshire.

ALEX. Of course. All-boys school?

RUPERT. Of course

ALEX. Rugby tours?

RUPERT. Captain of the rugby tours

ALEX. Nickname?

RUPERT. Rupedog.

ALEX. Rapedog?

RUPERT. Rupe-dog… Stop thinking about rape.

ALEX. Bet you had loads of dogs.

RUPERT. We did

ALEX. I want to smoke so bad.

RUPERT. We're in a… /

ALEX. I know.

RUPERT. And my asthma used to be quite… / sensitive

ALEX. Sensitive

RUPERT. Yes, the smallest thing could set it off again.

ALEX. Gosh, you must live in constant fear

RUPERT. I do.

ALEX. How you managed with all those dogs, I'll never know.

RUPERT. They had short hair.

ALEX. They

RUPERT. Mum bred them.

ALEX. Course she did, Labs?

RUPERT. Nope

ALEX. Beagles?

RUPERT. Bluetick Coonhounds.

ALEX. Excuse me

RUPERT. Bluetick Coonhounds, they're American, the official
    dog of Tennessee.

ALEX. This is ridiculous

RUPERT. George Washington had one.
    They have an unusual bark it's described as 'The Bells of
    Moscow'

ALEX. An accurate description?

RUPERT. Not really, more the 'Howl of Moscow'.

ALEX. Do it.

RUPERT. What? No.

ALEX. Go on do it. Howl for me, I want to imagine what it was
    like being you as a child

RUPERT. I'm not going to howl, we're in a /...

ALEX. A non-smoking area

RUPERT. In a public area.

ALEX. But not a non-howling area. Do it.

RUPERT. No.

ALEX. Okay I will

RUPERT. No. No don't

    Too late, she does.

    Ahhh, where is that wine?

ALEX. Was that accurate?

RUPERT. Noo. NO.

ALEX. Shall I go again

RUPERT. Everyone is looking

ALEX. So?

RUPERT. Everyone is looking at us

ALEX. This is promising.

RUPERT. Is it?

ALEX. I'm embarrassing you, like really embarrassing you

RUPERT. Yup.

ALEX. And you're going nowhere.

RUPERT. I could leave.

ALEX. Go on then...

RUPERT. Do you want me to?

ALEX. You won't.

RUPERT. How do you know?

ALEX. You're too nice

RUPERT. Nice, God.

ALEX. Nice is good.

RUPERT. Nice is boring

ALEX. Go on then, excite me...

RUPERT. What if I...

ALEX. What?

RUPERT. Oh I don't know...

ALEX. This is exciting

RUPERT. Insult you.

ALEX. Insult me...?

RUPERT. Your nose

ALEX. My nose...

RUPERT. It's very / ...

ALEX. What's wrong with my nose

RUPERT. Long

ALEX. Long?

RUPERT. Long

ALEX. God

Beat.

RUPERT. In a good way

ALEX. Oh right, great

RUPERT. In like a really good way

ALEX. Is it really long?

RUPERT. Has no one said that before

ALEX. No!

RUPERT. Oh

ALEX. Is it too long?

RUPERT. It's elegant

ALEX. You should have led with that

RUPERT. I should have I'm sorry

ALEX. It's okay

RUPERT. I really am sorry

ALEX. It's fine

RUPERT. I think your nose is just / great

ALEX. Long

RUPERT. No great, it's a great nose

Pause.

I'm sorry

ALEX. Stop saying sorry

RUPERT. Okay

Pause.

I am sorry

ALEX. I don't care.

RUPERT. I'm a twerp

ALEX *smirks*.

I'm such a twerp

ALEX. What a way to excite a woman

RUPERT. I'm normally a lot smoother

ALEX. Are you?

RUPERT. I'm normally incredibly smooth

ALEX. Smooth and rich what a catch

RUPERT. I'm not rich

ALEX. You look it

RUPERT. No I don't

ALEX. Look at your suit

RUPERT. I'm not rich-rich

ALEX. But you're clearly earning well

RUPERT. I'm doing alright

ALEX. More than alright, how much was that

She points at his watch.

RUPERT. That was a present

ALEX. From your mum

RUPERT. Yes. Of course

ALEX. Money makes people do weird things

RUPERT. Like what?

ALEX. Like shit on a mirror.

RUPERT. Do you know someone who has done that?

ALEX. All I know is it makes you bored and makes you mad.

RUPERT. Money keeps us safe.

ALEX. From what?

RUPERT. From everything.

ALEX. Not everything

RUPERT. Everything

ALEX. From cancer?

RUPERT. Yes. If my mum gets cancer I can afford her the best care, the best care imaginable.

ALEX. She's lucky

RUPERT. No, I am.

ALEX. You're such a Mummy's boy

RUPERT. Is that a problem?

ALEX. Does she still do your ironing?

RUPERT. No.

ALEX. Change your sheets?

RUPERT. No. My maid does all that.

Pause.

I'm joking.

ALEX. Are you?

RUPERT. Yes.

ALEX. I think they've forgotten our wine

RUPERT. It seems that way

ALEX. Punish me for smoking I expect

RUPERT. You deserve it. Filthy habit.

ALEX. Does your mum hate smoking?

RUPERT. Yes

ALEX. Would your mum hate me

RUPERT. Why? Are you planning on meeting her?

ALEX. No. Just wondered.

Beat.

RUPERT. Do you want to smoke?

ALEX. No

RUPERT. If you do we can leave

ALEX. I'm fine

RUPERT. We can just stand on the street and you can smoke if you want.

ALEX. I'm fine.

RUPERT. I wouldn't mind, not at all.

ALEX. What about your senstive asthma.

RUPERT. I'd risk it for you

ALEX. You'd risk death for me.

RUPERT. I would

ALEX. You barely know me

RUPERT. I'm a gentleman

ALEX. I can see the wine coming, you continue to live another day Rupert the Bear.

RUPERT. Phew. That was close.

Beat.

ALEX. I had a maid

RUPERT. Oh

ALEX. When I was growing up

RUPERT. How lovely

ALEX. My parents are stinking rich

RUPERT. Well, that's nice

ALEX. It's not

RUPERT. Okay

ALEX. And they hate smoking

RUPERT. Ah

ALEX. I kind of hate smoking.

RUPERT. Don't do it then

ALEX. But it really pisses them off

Beat.

RUPERT. I used to draw on walls

ALEX. Criminal

RUPERT. That would really piss off my mum

ALEX. Apart from that were you the perfect son?

RUPERT. Oh no

ALEX. No?

RUPERT. When I first lived with her, I'd have moments

ALEX. Moments?

RUPERT. Episodes, tantrums. Violent sometimes. Mum would put on music, really loudly, not the kind of music you're thinking. It was big old-school drum-and-bass music. She would turn it up, so loud, so loud, I could see the speakers bouncing, I could feel the floor shaking. And she'd say Dance. DANCE. DANCE DANCE RUPERT! And we'd dance.

ALEX. Then what?

RUPERT. All would be well.

ALEX. Do you still do it?

RUPERT. Yeah. Sometimes, not that much. I might do it tonight.

ALEX. Are you close to a moment?

RUPERT. I am.

ALEX. Am I that awful?

RUPERT. No. God no.
    I think you're...

ALEX. What?

RUPERT. Magnificent

ALEX. Apart from my long nose

RUPERT. Your very elegant nose

Beat.

ALEX. My dad had affairs

RUPERT. I'm sorry.

ALEX. And Cynthia's a bitch.

RUPERT. Cynthia?

ALEX. My mum

RUPERT. That's shit

ALEX. You swore Rupert the Bear.

RUPERT. I do swear on occasion.

ALEX. When it's necessary?

RUPERT. When necessary.

Beat.

ALEX. I like the wine

RUPERT. You do?

ALEX. I do

RUPERT. Apples?

ALEX. No, but definitely toothpaste.

*

RUPERT. I won't bang on, I could. Maybe I should. Tell you all about the dinners, the first fights, the parents, the holidays, the socks in the bed, the loose change under the sofa.
She never opens her post, is that important for you to know? Never opens it, then one day I did, and the next day I did it again until soon I always opened her post. And it became a thing. A thing we did. I could spend hours talking about the little things. They slowly build one on top of each other until soon they make a life. That's special I think, it happens slowly without realising without really planning. And I never expected that, expected any of that. How can something happen without a plan? All my life I've been planned, I've known the dates, the times, the journeys. But with Alex...

Scene Four

ALEX. It's a girl.

RUPERT. It is?

ALEX. Yes

RUPERT. I thought we / weren't going to…

ALEX. I changed my mind

RUPERT. When?

ALEX. Today, I rang

RUPERT. Right. Well you could have / …

ALEX. It's a girl!

RUPERT. A girl!

ALEX. Rose

RUPERT. Oh

ALEX. That's what we agreed

RUPERT. Yes.

ALEX. Rose

RUPERT. I know

ALEX. Rose

RUPERT. It's nice, it's a bit / you know

ALEX. A bit what?

RUPERT. A bit flowery

ALEX. It's a type of flower

RUPERT. I know

ALEX. We agreed

RUPERT. I know

ALEX. So what's the problem?

RUPERT. There isn't a problem

Pause.

It's just

ALEX. What?

RUPERT. It's just.

ALEX. What?

RUPERT. Do we want her / to be flowery

ALEX. We decided it was a good theme

RUPERT. Theme

ALEX. Yes a theme for our children's names

RUPERT. What?

ALEX. We did decide

Beat.

RUPERT. It's wet

ALEX. Wet?

RUPERT. It's a bit wet.

ALEX. A bit wet?

RUPERT. Princessy

ALEX. A flowery name / doesn't make her princessy

RUPERT. Do we want her to be princessy?

ALEX. No / but if she…

RUPERT. To have no backbone?

ALEX. To have no backbone?

RUPERT. I just worry, is all, your name says a lot about you

ALEX. You're named after a bear

RUPERT. Exactly / bears are

ALEX. A teddy bear!

Beat.

RUPERT. I never liked it

ALEX. What?

RUPERT. I've never liked it

ALEX. But we agreed

RUPERT. We didn't

ALEX. We did

RUPERT. I don't remember

ALEX. You do

Beat.

You do remember

RUPERT. What about Ethel?

ALEX. Ethel?

RUPERT. Yes

ALEX. No

Beat.

RUPERT. I don't like it

ALEX. But we agreed

RUPERT. We didn't agree

ALEX. We did

RUPERT. I do not remember any of this.

ALEX. We talked about having a 'Flower Bed' our very own flower bed.

RUPERT. We did not talk about that

ALEX. WE DID

RUPERT. Maybe you talked about it to yourself

ALEX. Excuse me?

RUPERT. Maybe you imagined you had that conversation

ALEX. I did not.

RUPERT. It wouldn't be the first time

ALEX. It would

RUPERT. Since you've… you know…

ALEX. Been pregnant

RUPERT. Yeah

ALEX. With our child

RUPERT. It wouldn't be the first time since you've been pregnant that you've had imaginary conversations

ALEX. I've never had an imaginary conversation

RUPERT. You have

ALEX. Name one then

RUPERT. In bed the other night

ALEX. In our bed.

RUPERT. Yes in our bed.

ALEX. What was I saying?

RUPERT. It doesn't matter

ALEX. No say.

RUPERT. All sorts of stuff

ALEX. What stuff?

RUPERT. Just stuff.

ALEX. Well I was obviously talking to you

RUPERT. You weren't, I wasn't in the room.

ALEX. Where were you?

RUPERT. I got up to go for a wee

ALEX. Don't say wee you know I hate it when you say wee.

RUPERT. Okay, whatever, anyway, I got up, I wasn't in the room and then.

ALEX. Then what?

RUPERT. I came back and you were talking

ALEX. What was I saying?

RUPERT. You were saying, you know

ALEX. I don't

RUPERT. Sexy stuff

ALEX. Well obviously I was talking to you

RUPERT. No! I was doing a wee.

ALEX. Don't say wee

RUPERT. You were not talking to me.

ALEX. Okay, then I was talking in my sleep

RUPERT. You were sex-talking in your sleep

ALEX. Okay, I was sex-talking in my sleep

RUPERT. There you go

ALEX. There you go what?

RUPERT. You're having conversations with someone who isn't there.

ALEX. No, I'm having conversations with people who are very much there.

Beat.

RUPERT. People

Beat.

People

ALEX. Yes

Beat.

RUPERT. What people?

ALEX. Just, all sorts

RUPERT. All sorts

ALEX. YES.

RUPERT. Not me?

ALEX. No, not really

RUPERT. Sometimes though?

ALEX. Actually no, not really ever

RUPERT. Who are these people?

ALEX. I don't know they don't have faces

RUPERT. Why?

ALEX. They just don't

RUPERT. Everyone has a face

ALEX. Not these people

RUPERT. Why?

ALEX. They're wearing things

RUPERT. What do you mean?

ALEX. Wearing things on their face.

RUPERT. Things?

ALEX. Yes

RUPERT. What do you mean things on their face?

ALEX. You know what I mean Rupert

RUPERT. No I don't Alex

ALEX. Sexy things

RUPERT. Sexy things

ALEX. Yes

RUPERT. Like what

ALEX. Balaclavas

RUPERT. Balaclavas

ALEX. Yes, and they're French

RUPERT. What?

ALEX. Usually they're French with balaclavas and I'm tied up.

RUPERT. You never let me tie you up.

ALEX. Yeah, but it's you.

RUPERT. Thanks

ALEX. You're cuddly not sexy

RUPERT. I am sexy

ALEX. You say wee, saying wee isn't sexy

RUPERT. French people say wee all the time.

ALEX. It's not the same

RUPERT. Okay well I'll stop

ALEX. That's not the point

 Beat.

 I love having sex with you

RUPERT. I can be sexy

ALEX. I know

RUPERT (*in a French accent*). I can be very sexy

 Beat.

 I don't like Rose

ALEX. But we agreed

RUPERT. I don't remember agreeing

ALEX. You did I promise

RUPERT. Yeah, but I never thought it would...

ALEX. Would what?

RUPERT. I never thought it would be a girl

ALEX. Oh

RUPERT. I was like ninety-nine per cent sure it would be a boy

ALEX. Right

RUPERT. So I'm actually rather…

ALEX. How were you so sure?

RUPERT. I just had a feeling

ALEX. What do you mean you had a 'feeling'

RUPERT. Just a, you know, manly feeling

ALEX. A manly feeling?

RUPERT. Yeah.

ALEX. Right

RUPERT. I had a manly feeling Alex

ALEX. That's fine Rupert

RUPERT. I just felt

ALEX. Manly

RUPERT. No I felt / like I had…

ALEX. How were you so sure Rupert?

RUPERT. As I was saying. Alex. On the day we conceived / it

ALEX. The 19th of October

RUPERT. The 19th of October

ALEX. And. Stop calling it 'it'.

RUPERT. I'm not calling it Rose

ALEX. We'll see. So on the 19th of October

RUPERT. On the day we conceived…

ALEX. Rose

RUPERT. Oh it doesn't matter

ALEX. What?

RUPERT. It doesn't matter

ALEX. No what?

RUPERT. You always interrupt

ALEX. I don't

RUPERT. You do, you asked me to tell you and I'm trying / and you keep interrupting

ALEX. I'm sorry I'll stop

Beat.

RUPERT. So, on the day we conceived / the baby

ALEX. Rose!

RUPERT. Alex

ALEX. Sorry!

RUPERT. I remember when I... ended

ALEX. Came

RUPERT. Finished

ALEX. Jizzed

RUPERT. Finalised the seed of our baby

ALEX. Jesus Christ!

RUPERT. It was like a really big...

ALEX. What?

RUPERT. It was a lot of... / sperm

ALEX. Sperm?

RUPERT. And I remember thinking, cor that's a big load, that's a manly load

ALEX. So it must be a boy

RUPERT. Yes, boys are generally bigger

ALEX. No, no they're not.

RUPERT. They are, they have bigger bones

ALEX. Sperm doesn't affect bones

RUPERT. I just had a feeling that I had ejected, if you were going to get pregnant from my ejection /

ALEX. Rupert

RUPERT. / That I had ejected a boy into you

ALEX. This is charming

RUPERT. Sorry

ALEX. This is really rather odd. Quite / uncomfortable with it all
actually

RUPERT. So, yeah, I am actually very very shocked / that it's a
girl

ALEX. So am I.
A Rose

RUPERT. Not Rose

ALEX. A Rose amongst two thorns.

Scene Five

ALEX. I'd like yellow

RUPERT. Okay

ALEX. Oh

RUPERT. Do you not want yellow?

ALEX. I really do

RUPERT. Then why do you sound disappointed?

ALEX. I'd thought you'd say no

RUPERT. Why?

ALEX. We always disagree, I thought we would disagree on this

RUPERT. I think yellow is great, / neutral

ALEX. Neutral

RUPERT. Great minds.

ALEX. Indeed

Beat.

This is weird

RUPERT. What?

ALEX. Deciding something quickly with you

RUPERT. It's normal

ALEX. Oh this is what normal feels like

RUPERT. Yes, I guess so, it's nice isn't it?

ALEX. Very grown-up.

RUPERT. It's like we're parents

ALEX. Nearly, not quite parenting yet.

Pause.

She'll have a great mind won't she?

RUPERT. Of course

ALEX. A great mind, a creative mind, a mathematical mind, a dirty mind.

RUPERT. Not a dirty mind

ALEX. Why not?

RUPERT. I don't want my daughter to have a dirty mind

ALEX. Well she will

RUPERT. Stop it

ALEX. She was made in sin, I bet she'll be filthy

RUPERT. Can you not talk about our baby like that.

ALEX. Our bastard baby

RUPERT. Alex

ALEX. What? It's important to be curious

RUPERT. I hope she's always a virgin

ALEX. That's awful

RUPERT. It's not

ALEX. You're not a virgin

RUPERT. That's different

ALEX. I'm not a virgin

RUPERT. It's different

ALEX. Why? Sex is important, I want her to have it, and be good at it. I want her to know what good sex is. We have to be able to talk to her, guide her, advise her.

RUPERT. Advise her

ALEX. Yes

RUPERT. On what? Blowjobs?

ALEX. Maybe yes.

RUPERT. What sit her down with a can of Pledge and show her what's what

ALEX. A can of Pledge?

RUPERT. Yes

ALEX. Bloody hell

RUPERT. What?

ALEX. A can of Pledge seriously

RUPERT. Everyone has Pledge in their cupboards

ALEX. It's quite in-your-face, it's quite intimidating

RUPERT. It's more or less the same shape

ALEX. IT IS NOT

RUPERT. It is, it's long and cylindrical

ALEX. Wooooo

RUPERT. I think it would be good for a demonstration.

Beat.

ALEX. Is that what you think you look like?

RUPERT. No! No!

ALEX. You sure?

RUPERT. Yes I mean no, no, no, I don't think. No.

ALEX. Good because you don't

RUPERT. I know

ALEX. You're not even close

RUPERT. I'm above average.

ALEX. You're not a can of Pledge.

   Beat.

   You have to be able to talk to her about these things, even if it
   makes you feel uncomfortable.

RUPERT. I won't ever

ALEX. That's selfish

RUPERT. It's not

ALEX. Imagine if a boy asks her to do something because it's
   meant to be cool.

RUPERT. Like what?

ALEX. Like anal.

RUPERT. No one is going to tell her that she has to do... that in
   order to be cool.

ALEX. They might, and if we don't build that openness, that
   conversation from the get-go, then she won't know and that'll
   be it.

RUPERT. That'll be what?

ALEX. She'll have anal and she won't ever know if she's okay
   with it.

   Beat.

RUPERT. Maybe we should stick with white

ALEX. Fine don't talk about it

RUPERT. Or cream

ALEX. No.

RUPERT. It's less suggestive

ALEX. Than yellow

RUPERT. Less oppressive

ALEX. Than a neutral yellow

RUPERT. Yeah, exactly. Yellow might make her...

ALEX. What?

RUPERT. Might make her

ALEX. What Rupert?

RUPERT. Might make her like anal.

Scene Six

ALEX. Let's move

RUPERT. Where?

ALEX. The countryside

RUPERT. What would we do?

ALEX. Be bored I suppose

RUPERT. Exactly

ALEX. I'd like to be bored, it would be easier

RUPERT. We could never go to the theatre

ALEX. When do we ever go to the theatre?

RUPERT. Well, if we wanted to go it would be harder.

ALEX. Let's risk it.

RUPERT. What about work?

ALEX. Maybe I won't go back.

RUPERT. Why?

ALEX. I hate it, you know I hate it.

RUPERT. But the money

ALEX. Will just go on childcare

Beat.

RUPERT. We could have an allotment

ALEX. Yes

RUPERT. Grow stuff

ALEX. Carrots

*

RUPERT. We're going to be poor

ALEX. No we're not

RUPERT. We're going to really struggle.

ALEX. We'll be fine

RUPERT. I mean it

ALEX. Okay

RUPERT. We won't make enough money

ALEX. Okay

RUPERT. So we're going to struggle

ALEX. I get it

RUPERT. Do you Alex?

ALEX. I DO!

RUPERT. I just don't feel like you're engaging

ALEX. I am.

RUPERT. Alex

ALEX. What?

RUPERT. Can you just please / just…

ALEX. What?

*

ALEX. We can make small changes. I've made a list of some small changes.

RUPERT. Are those my socks?

ALEX. These socks?

RUPERT. The socks on your feet

ALEX. Yes

RUPERT. Don't wear my socks Alex

ALEX. Rupert can we not?

RUPERT. Get your own socks

ALEX. I prefer yours

RUPERT. I love those socks, I've been looking for them. They're my soft socks.

ALEX. You done?

RUPERT. You know they're my soft socks.

ALEX. I know

RUPERT. You know I don't like you wearing them

ALEX. I was cold

RUPERT. Wear your own.

ALEX. Can we not? I've made a list.

RUPERT. Wear your own / socks Alex

ALEX. I've made a list of some small / changes Rupert and I'd really like to share it with you

RUPERT. I find it frustrating when I can't find my things. / You know that.

ALEX. Yes

RUPERT. And usually when I can't find them, it's because you've taken them

ALEX. I've made a list Rupert

RUPERT. I don't want to hear it

ALEX. Cool.

RUPERT. I'm too angry.

*

ALEX. The gym. That's fifty quid each a month

RUPERT. Okay

ALEX. No?

RUPERT. Gym sure

ALEX. What?

RUPERT. You never use it, but I do, I use it a lot actually. Actually.

ALEX. You don't

RUPERT. I love the gym, it helps me.

ALEX. Helps you what?

RUPERT. Get through the week.

ALEX. You haven't been in six months

RUPERT. That's not true

ALEX. I rang to see how often you go and you haven't been in six months.

RUPERT. This month's been crazy

ALEX. More crazy than having a baby?

RUPERT. Fine

ALEX. You can go running

RUPERT. It's cold

ALEX. Then get fat, like me.
Sky TV that can go

RUPERT. Agreed

ALEX. *The Week* subscription

RUPERT. Never read it.

ALEX. We should

RUPERT. I know

ALEX. We should read more

RUPERT. I know

ALEX. We're very busy

RUPERT. Exactly

ALEX. Okay, *The Week* gone.
    We can do a bulk shop once a week

RUPERT. Online!

ALEX. Exciting!
    Cinema membership

RUPERT. You gave that to me, that's a present

ALEX. It's going, you've used it once.

RUPERT. I might use it again

ALEX. You used it to get a muffin

RUPERT....

ALEX. Yoga studio

RUPERT. I'm not a member of a yoga studio

ALEX. I am

RUPERT. When do you do yoga?

ALEX. I don't

RUPERT. How much is it?

ALEX. I'm not saying

RUPERT. Tell ME!

ALEX. No it's embarrassing, I'm embarrassed.

RUPERT. Is it a lot?

ALEX. It's a lot, it's so much

RUPERT. How much?

ALEX. If I tell you, you can't be cross.

RUPERT. I promise

ALEX. Promise?

RUPERT. Promise.

ALEX. I can't say

RUPERT. Say

ALEX. I can't say it out loud.

RUPERT. Write it down.

ALEX. Okay. (*Writes it down.*)

RUPERT. A month

*

ALEX. We'll freeze them all.

RUPERT. You made twelve

ALEX. Twelve lasagnes

RUPERT. We can't eat lasagne for twelve weeks

ALEX. It's quorn lasagne

RUPERT. It's so much quorn lasagne

ALEX. It's saving

RUPERT. It's boring

ALEX. It's for the baby

*

RUPERT. Where's the sourdough?

ALEX. There's sliced white in the cupboard.

RUPERT. What?

RUPERT. And the Lurpak

ALEX. Tesco's own, just as good.

*

RUPERT. I'd thought we'd stay with my mum.

ALEX. When?

RUPERT. In the summer

ALEX. God why?

RUPERT. Instead of a holiday.

ALEX. No

RUPERT. Why?

ALEX. It's damp

RUPERT. Not in the summer

ALEX. It's quite moist.

RUPERT. It's for the baby, we're saving.

ALEX. We could stay with my parents?

RUPERT. No, absolutely not

ALEX. Why

RUPERT. Cynthia will make me meditate.

ALEX. So.

RUPERT. I hate it

ALEX. You need it

RUPERT. She'll make me sleep with crystals again

ALEX. It'll do you some good.

RUPERT. Didn't do you any good.

ALEX. It did, I'm a very zen person. My chakras have always been aligned

RUPERT. Your crackers are not aligned.

ALEX. Chakras, not crackers.

RUPERT. I know.

ALEX. Oh...

RUPERT. It was a joke

ALEX. I don't get it

RUPERT. It was just a joke

ALEX. But I don't get it.

RUPERT. Crackers sounds like / chakras

ALEX. It doesn't

RUPERT. And Cynthia is crackers

ALEX. Right

RUPERT. It was a joke

ALEX. It was crap

RUPERT. Fine. I don't want to talk about it any more.

ALEX. It's not my fault it wasn't funny.

RUPERT. I don't want to stay with your parents. I can't do it, I hate it, there's no phone signal, no internet, there's barely electricity

ALEX. So?

RUPERT. It's like going back in time

ALEX. We can reconnect

RUPERT. What happens if there's an emergency?

ALEX. Like what?

RUPERT. Like a terrorist attack

ALEX. Well we'll be safe, we will be away from it

RUPERT. What happens if there's a terrorist attack and all our friends die

ALEX. I wouldn't mind if I'm honest...

RUPERT. Alex

ALEX. Oh Rupert they're all so boring, so smug and chatty, I hate the chattiness.

*

RUPERT. Why are you so red?

ALEX. I walked

RUPERT. From work?

ALEX. I thought it would be nice

RUPERT. You never walk.

ALEX. Cutting back Rupert

*

ALEX. I want pizza.

RUPERT. You've got lasagne

ALEX. I need pizza

RUPERT. It's expensive

ALEX. I want a sourdough pizza with a tomato and burrata salad.

RUPERT. You'll live.

ALEX. I won't

RUPERT. You can't have burrata anyway it's not pasteurised

ALEX. Oh piss off

*

RUPERT. Fuck

ALEX. What's that noise?

RUPERT. Fuck it.

ALEX. Rupert what is it?

RUPERT. It's the bloody boiler

ALEX. Turn it off

RUPERT. I can't

ALEX. Just turn it off

RUPERT. I can't Alex it's clearly broken.

ALEX. That bloody boiler.

*

ALEX. Everyone not just me.

RUPERT. Are you sure?

ALEX. Yes, they have no money.

RUPERT. How long have they known?

ALEX. A while

RUPERT. Are you sure it's everyone?

ALEX. Yes, not just me, the pregnant woman.

RUPERT. Well what are we going to do?

ALEX. I don't know

RUPERT. What about your maternity pay?

ALEX. There's no money

RUPERT. Savings?

ALEX. No

RUPERT. Why?

ALEX. I didn't make enough to have savings

RUPERT. I told you

ALEX. Yes

RUPERT. I told you you need to start saving

ALEX. Yes

RUPERT. Every month

ALEX. Right, well I didn't.

RUPERT. How did you not know?

ALEX. They kept it well hidden

RUPERT. You didn't even get a sense that they were in trouble

ALEX. No Rupert, I didn't get a sense.

RUPERT. I told you, put ten per cent aside each month

ALEX. Yes. You did

RUPERT. Did you?

ALEX. I've said that I didn't Rupert.

RUPERT. I don't understand this / how can you not have had a sense it was falling apart?

ALEX. Okay well I'm sorry it's so hard on you

RUPERT. You'll have to ask your parents?

ALEX. For what, a job?

RUPERT. No, money.

ALEX. Uh no Rupert, don't be silly.

RUPERT. I'm not being silly they're loaded

ALEX. They won't give us money

RUPERT. Why?

ALEX. They don't work like that you know they don't work like that.

RUPERT. Well what the fuck are you going to do?

ALEX. What are we going to do?

RUPERT. You Alex, you. I haven't lost my job.

ALEX. It's not my fault

RUPERT. You have no savings, no income from now on, no maternity pay, nothing, there is nothing, just what I earn.

ALEX. It's not my fault

RUPERT. It's never your fault

ALEX. This isn't my fault

RUPERT. FUCK'S SAKE ALEX

ALEX. Don't shout at me.

RUPERT. FUCK

ALEX. Don't swear Rupert

RUPERT. I'll SWEAR IF I WANT TO.

ALEX. Never shout at me. Shout at me like that again I'll leave.

Beat.

RUPERT. I don't earn enough money to support us

ALEX. You do

RUPERT. We don't have enough savings

ALEX. You earn shitloads

RUPERT. Ten per cent Alex… it's not much

ALEX. I'm sorry.

RUPERT. Christ on a bike Alex!

ALEX. Oh Rupert

RUPERT. What?

ALEX. Rupert

RUPERT. What?

ALEX. Here. (*Puts his hand on her stomach.*)

RUPERT. What? I can't feel anything

ALEX. She's kicking

RUPERT. Where?

ALEX. Here!

RUPERT. No I can't feel anything

ALEX. She's kicking all over the place

RUPERT. Well not for me. Perfect.

*

ALEX. Look!

RUPERT. Oh… it's pink

ALEX. It's a pink jumper

RUPERT. For what?

ALEX. A baby, our baby. I'm going to knit all her clothes

RUPERT. Are you a knitter?

ALEX. I'm not

RUPERT. What is it?

ALEX. A jumper I said

RUPERT. Oh right

ALEX. See?

*

ALEX. Rupert!
    Rupert!
    Oh my God, Rupert!

RUPERT. Hang on

ALEX. What are you doing?

RUPERT. I'm doing a wee.

ALEX. Don't say wee
    Hurry up.

RUPERT. What's wrong? Is it the baby?

ALEX. Guess

RUPERT. What's happened?

ALEX. Guess

RUPERT. I hate guessing Al, just tell me.

ALEX. Guess

RUPERT. I can't guess

ALEX. You can

RUPERT. I can't

ALEX. We won.

RUPERT. Won what?

ALEX. We won...

RUPERT. What?

Pause.

WHAT!!!

ALEX. We won the lottery

RUPERT. Good one Al

ALEX. No, no I mean it.

RUPERT. Right

ALEX. Honestly, we won Rupert, we won the lottery

Beat.

RUPERT. Nooo?

ALEX. Yes

RUPERT. Seriously

ALEX. Yes, my lucky numbers.

RUPERT. Have you just found out?

ALEX. Yes

RUPERT. Were you on the train?

ALEX. Yes

RUPERT. Were you sat down on the train?

ALEX. Yes

RUPERT. You were sat down on the train and then what?

ALEX. I checked the numbers

RUPERT. Yes...

ALEX. And then I was like GOD we've won!

RUPERT. Fuck

ALEX. Yes

RUPERT. This is huge

ALEX. Yes

RUPERT. Have we seriously won the lottery?

ALEX. We have YES!!!

RUPERT. Oh my God, oh my God. Have you told anyone

ALEX. No just you.

RUPERT. How much, how much is it?

Silence.

ALEX. Fifty quid

Beat.

Fifty smackeroons baby!

Beat.

RUPERT. We're rich

ALEX. Loaded

RUPERT. All our problems solved

ALEX. It's our lucky day!

RUPERT. Let's celebrate

ALEX. PIZZA

RUPERT. Sourdough

ALEX. Burrata

RUPERT. It's not pasteurised

ALEX. Fuck off Rupert

Scene Seven

RUPERT. A crisp morning in the navy suit with the red tie from
my school days that I should have forgotten but that I keep to
remind me of success. My shoes polished like my
grandfather's and an umbrella tucked neatly under my arm just
in case. Green skirt ironed in a rush with straighteners, a pink
and yellow jumper clashing but in a charming way. She is
absentmindedly eating from a pot of raspberry Tiptree, her hair

still in a towel despite being fully dressed and she is casually scrolling through her phone. I walk past and tap her nose heading towards my breakfast, on a place mat with yesterday's newspaper beside it.

My breakfast is half-eaten!

ALEX. What?

RUPERT. You ate my breakfast.

ALEX. The baby ate it.

RUPERT. You have toothpaste on your jumper.

ALEX. Oh it's been there for years

RUPERT. Do you ever wash?

ALEX. Will you ever go to work?

RUPERT. Goodbye you

ALEX. Goodbye me.

Beat.

Oh

RUPERT. What?

ALEX. I don't know

Scene Eight

ALEX. I don't like her.

RUPERT. You haven't got a choice

ALEX. She's judging me.

RUPERT. She's not judging you.

ALEX. When I asked for jelly she sighed

RUPERT. She did not

ALEX. She did

RUPERT. You haven't even eaten your jelly

ALEX. I hate it

RUPERT. Eat it

ALEX. I hate it

RUPERT. I'll eat it

ALEX. No I might want it

*

ALEX. I can't

RUPERT. You have to

ALEX. I can't

RUPERT. Where is she?

ALEX. Go find her

RUPERT. Okay

ALEX. No come back.

*

ALEX. Why is she speaking like that?

RUPERT. Like what?

ALEX. In that weird way

RUPERT. She's got an accent Alex

ALEX. I can't understand her

RUPERT. Shall I interpret?

ALEX. Don't be so fucking irritating Rupert!

RUPERT. Don't be so fucking racist Alex!

*

ALEX. Okay

RUPERT. Okay

ALEX. Okay

RUPERT. You're amazing

ALEX. Don't touch me

RUPERT. I love you

ALEX. Shut up

RUPERT. You're so amazing

ALEX. Shut up Rupert.

RUPERT. I love you so much

ALEX. Rupert

RUPERT. You're so incredible

ALEX. Fuck off, fuck off, fuck, off fuck off, FUCK OFF.

*

ALEX. She's early

RUPERT. It's fine

ALEX. It's too soon

RUPERT. It's nice to be early, all the best people come early

*

ALEX. Where's the midwife?

RUPERT. She's here

ALEX. Do you think she knows we haven't bought a car seat and that's why she hates us?

RUPERT. She doesn't hate us

ALEX. She does

RUPERT. Anyway I'm going to buy one.

ALEX. Oh God okay

RUPERT. Take a breath

ALEX. No I can't

RUPERT. Just a little breath

ALEX. Okay

RUPERT. Breathe

ALEX. Okay

RUPERT. Keep breathing

ALEX. I am fucking breathing.

RUPERT. The second before your life changes everything slows down, I slowly pull her hair back, she grabs my hand and squeezes and squeezes but I don't feel it, I don't feel the pain. I just watch her as this magnificent fucking crazy woman fucking rocks the room. And everything stops for one moment and she looks at me and we stare at each other and wait, wait for the sound of the first

ALEX. Crying, why isn't she crying?

RUPERT. It's a boy

ALEX. What?

RUPERT. It's a bloody boy, I told you it was a boy.

ALEX. No we were told it was a girl?

RUPERT. A mistake, we've got a baby boy

ALEX. A boy?

RUPERT. A boy!

ALEX. Not Rose

RUPERT. NO!

ALEX. A boy. I love him

RUPERT. I told you!

ALEX. You did.

RUPERT. Didn't I tell you it was a boy?

ALEX. You did, you did, you're so clever.

Where is she?

RUPERT. He not she

ALEX. Where is he?

RUPERT. They're just

ALEX. Can I have him?

RUPERT. Let's get him shall we?

ALEX. Why isn't he crying?
  Where is he?

RUPERT. Don't get up

ALEX. I want him.

RUPERT. Alex stop trying to get up.

ALEX. He isn't crying Rupert

RUPERT. I know

ALEX. What's happened?

RUPERT. I don't know, I don't understand.

ALEX. Where is he?

RUPERT. It's fine

ALEX. It's not

RUPERT. It is, they're just

ALEX. I want my baby

RUPERT. Excuse me what is happening?

ALEX. Why isn't he crying

She tries to get up.

RUPERT. Alex don't get up.

ALEX. Get off me, give me my baby.

RUPERT. Don't get up.

Beat.

I um.
I just.

I didn't do anything... that helpful.

Because it's... you can't help, I couldn't do anything helpful. I stood at the bottom of the bed and held her foot. I was still in my suit, I still had my tie on. I'd bought my umbrella just in case.

Twenty-three hours later at 8:15 p.m., room nineteen, third floor, six pounds five ounces, ten fingers, ten toes. Perfect.

ALEX. Rupert why isn't he?
    Rupert?
    Rupert?
    Rupert why isn't he crying?

RUPERT. Alex

ALEX. Why isn't he crying?

RUPERT. I don't know.

ALEX. Can I see him?

RUPERT. I don't know.

ALEX. What's wrong with / my baby?

RUPERT. I don't know

ALEX. You do

RUPERT. I don't

ALEX. Please can you make him cry?

RUPERT. I can't

ALEX. Please can you make him cry?

RUPERT. I can't

ALEX. Please.

    Silence.

Scene Nine

RUPERT. A crisp morning, a black suit with a black tie bought
the day before. Shoes polished like my grandfather's and an
umbrella waiting by the door.
A black polo-neck with a black skirt, hair brushed straight
unlike the usual messy bun, two pearl earrings and a necklace
placed gently around her neck, that I secure with difficulty.
Her tights have a hole in them, but it's too late by the time I've
pulled them up I don't have the energy to take them off her.
Shall I tie your hair up?
I can do a mean French plait
Which shoes?
The car will be here soon
I think in about ten minutes
It might be here already actually, I'll have a look.
I've got your coat, your fur one, well fake-fur one. Shall I put
it on, c'mon sit up my love, there you go and give me your
arm we'll pop it through.
Which shoes?
It's cold, it's surprisingly cold for this time of year I'll find
your boots. You might need some woolly socks, have a
rummage in my drawer, take mine.

ALEX. I'm not allowed

RUPERT. What?

ALEX. I'm not allowed, you don't like me taking your socks?

RUPERT. I don't mind

ALEX. You do, you get cross when I steal them.

RUPERT. Only because they never come back matching

ALEX. So why are you letting me take them now?

RUPERT. Because
    Because
    I don't want your feet to get cold

ALEX. Okay

RUPERT. I want you to wear my socks

ALEX. Okay

RUPERT. I'll get your shoes.

ALEX. Okay

He comes back with her boots.

RUPERT. Here we go, give me your first foot, there we go my love.

ALEX. Stop it

RUPERT. What?

ALEX. That

RUPERT. What?

ALEX. Talking to me like I'm her

Beat.

RUPERT. We have to give him a name

ALEX. Her

RUPERT. No him, a baby boy Alex, we had a baby boy.

ALEX. Rose

RUPERT. Alex it was a boy.

ALEX. It.

RUPERT. He

ALEX. HER. ROSE

RUPERT. It's the wrong name.

ALEX. She's not alive she doesn't know

RUPERT. We had a baby boy

ALEX. We didn't

RUPERT. We have to put a name on the, I need you to tell me what name you want to put on the gravestone. I need to tell them.

ALEX. Rose

RUPERT. We can't put Rose

ALEX. Why?

RUPERT. We can't

ALEX. You did, you put that name on the death certificate

RUPERT. I know but

ALEX. So why can't we put it on the gravestone?

RUPERT. Alex, please. Please.

Beat.

The car is here, it's been here for half an hour Alex. We have to go.

ALEX. I'm ready.

They go to leave.

RUPERT. They want to know if you want to hold the coffin on your lap, on the way.

ALEX. Is she in it?

RUPERT. He is.

ALEX. I can hold her?

RUPERT. In the coffin yes

ALEX. Yes.

RUPERT. Okay, you'll sit down and they'll place him on your lap.

ALEX. Will he know?

RUPERT. Sorry?

ALEX. Will he know I'm holding him?

RUPERT. Yes.
Of course he will.

ALEX. He'll know I'm there?

RUPERT. Yes.

ALEX. Really.

RUPERT. Yes.

*

ALEX. Edward
     Edward

RUPERT. Edward

ALEX. Teddy

RUPERT. Like a bear

ALEX. Like a bear

RUPERT. Like Rupert

ALEX. Yes.

Scene Ten

ALEX. A crisp morning, a pink onesie covered in yellow stars, a
     purple cardigan that clashed horribly, but it's all they had and I
     didn't want you to be cold my love. Socks so small that when I
     took them out of the packet I thought, these won't fit. But they
     did. Perfectly. A blue beanie, knitted but in a charming way. A
     grey comforter folded under your head, a teddy bear tucked in
     beside you, and his red tie secretly hidden under the blanket.
     You have his nose. You have your daddy's nose.
     I'm going to paint your room. I'm going to decorate your
     nursery. I'm going to fill it with stars.
     Daddy won't like that, Daddy will hate that, I think Daddy
     may hate me.
     People bring food to my door, literally. People I don't even
     know or like come to my door, present me with a hotpot, a
     Thermos of soup, endless fucking brownies and then they
     come back a day later and pick it up and ask what I'd like
     next, what takes your fancy? They don't ask me how I am,
     they don't even know your name. I just want them to say your
     name.

     So I spice it up, I spend hours researching difficult meals,
     curries with obscure spices, or a passion fruit and papaya pie, a
     twelve-hour beef stew. They do it, they cook it all, these
     people who now feel they know me. That they know you.

I want to know what you look like, I want to hear your laugh I want to hear your cry. I want to pick up your sock and test the temperature of your bath with my elbow. I want, I want to have your comforter permanently thrown over my shoulder and I want to manically search the flat for your lost toy that you just can't sleep without. I bought so much Tupperware so that I could have chopped-up carrots on me like a mum, like a real mum. I hate myself, Christ I'm a fucking cliché who talks to her dead baby. Why hasn't the earth stopped turning, why aren't buildings collapsing? Where are the alarms and the police and the army? How can there still be sun when you didn't get a chance to feel it on your face? Why was it you? Where did you go?

Scene Eleven

RUPERT. You're painting

ALEX. Yes

RUPERT. That's excellent

ALEX. Thank you

RUPERT. What are you painting?

ALEX. Teddy's room.

RUPERT. Okay

He notices the colour of the room.

You're painting it yellow.

ALEX. You see we never decided

RUPERT. On what?

ALEX. We never decided on the colour

RUPERT. No I guess not.

ALEX. We never decided on the colour of his room.

RUPERT. I know

ALEX. We never decided on his name

RUPERT. Okay

ALEX. We hadn't even bought a car seat.

RUPERT. I know

ALEX. So we obviously weren't planning on taking him home

RUPERT....

ALEX. We hadn't decided on a colour or a name or bought him anything to travel in.

RUPERT. I was going to

ALEX. Going to

RUPERT. Yes

ALEX. Always going to.

> RUPERT *notices a bag full of teddies and toys and things to decorate a nursery, he hasn't seen them before, they're recently purchased.*

RUPERT. What are these?

ALEX. Toys

RUPERT. And these?

ALEX. They're toys Rupert

RUPERT. I mean these Alex, these pictures and decorations. What's this?

ALEX. It's a lampshade.

RUPERT. I know, why is it here?

ALEX. I bought it today, I bought it all today.

RUPERT. Why?

ALEX. For the nursery

> *Beat.*

RUPERT. How did you pay for it?

ALEX. With money

RUPERT. What money?

ALEX. My money

RUPERT. You don't have money

ALEX. Cynthia gave me some

RUPERT. Your mum

ALEX. Don't say mum

Beat.

RUPERT. When did you see Cynthia?

ALEX. I didn't?

RUPERT. So when did you get the money?

ALEX. She sent a credit card

RUPERT. Right

ALEX. Is that okay?

Beat.

RUPERT. Okay

ALEX. I told you I'm painting it.

RUPERT. Yes, you said.

Beat.

Have you eaten?

ALEX. No

RUPERT. Shall I cook?

ALEX. Okay

RUPERT. Do we have any veg?

ALEX. I think there is some frozen veg in the freezer

RUPERT. The school-dinner veg?

ALEX. Yes

> RUPERT *heads into the kitchen. He goes to the freezer and he finds a frozen lasagne, with 'For the First Night' written on it. He holds the lasagne tightly, not minding how cold it is, how it is ruining his suit. He then puts it back in the freezer.*

RUPERT. I don't want you to paint the room

ALEX. Why?

RUPERT. It's

ALEX. It's

RUPERT. Wrong

ALEX. Why?

RUPERT. I don't want you to paint the room.

> ALEX *continues to paint.*

> Stop it

> *She keeps painting.*

> Stop it

> *She continues to paint.*

> I know you can hear me will you just stop please, Alex. Alex?

ALEX. We didn't decide on a colour

RUPERT. I know.

ALEX. We didn't get a car seat.

RUPERT. I know

ALEX. We didn't even decide on a name

RUPERT. I know

ALEX. So no wonder.

RUPERT. No wonder what?

ALEX. No wonder he decided to die

> *Beat.*

RUPERT. Stop painting

She doesn't stop.

Alex please

She keeps going.

Will you stop!

ALEX *continues to paint, ignoring him, he goes over and grabs her arms, holds them tightly, she fights back, but he is stronger and he pulls the roller out of her hands. They stand and look at each other.* ALEX *then goes back to the tray and scoops some paint into her hands. She throws it at the wall then starts spreading it around.* RUPERT *stands there, watching her and holding the roller.*

Scene Twelve

ALEX. I went to a coffee shop today. I wore Daddy's big puffa jacket and ordered a fresh mint tea. Not because I wanted one I just panicked and ordered the most expensive thing on the menu. I felt everyone staring so I thought if I order the most expensive thing they will think I'm okay.
It's funny when it happened I was so scared about having to tell people, close but no cigar that sort of thing, but actually it was really easy, because one day you're pregnant and the next day you're not and if there is no baby, well then they know. Daddy suggested sending a card out.
Okay I thought. That'll be nice. So I bought hundreds of Peter Rabbit cards from Paperchase with 'It's A Boy' written on the top. I crossed out 'A Boy' and wrote 'Dead' instead, 'It's Dead'. 'It's Dead, All Our Love, Alex and Rupert' then I posted them, first-class.
You were so little Teddy. I held your little feet in my hands and kissed your toes and thought about how little you were, how little and unnecessary you are in this massive world. Just a blip in the universe. No one cares, really. That's the truth.

Scene Thirteen

ALEX. What are these?

RUPERT. Nothing.

He goes to take them off her.

ALEX. No, what are they?

RUPERT. They're adoption papers

ALEX. I can see

RUPERT. My mum sent them.

ALEX. Okay

RUPERT. My mum sent them all.

ALEX. Why are you talking to her?

RUPERT. I talk to her every day

ALEX. Why?

RUPERT. She's my mum.

ALEX. Don't say that.

RUPERT. What?

ALEX. That?

RUPERT. What?

ALEX. Stop saying mum.

Beat.

RUPERT. It's nothing.

ALEX. It's a whole file.

RUPERT. It's the research from when she adopted me

ALEX. You're thirty-five

RUPERT. I know

ALEX. So this stuff is ancient, it won't be, it won't... I don't
    understand why she is sending this?

RUPERT. She's trying to help. C'mon, Alex

ALEX. What?

RUPERT. She's my mum

ALEX. She's not, you're adopted

RUPERT....

ALEX. She's not your mum. She can't get pregnant. She'll never be one.

Beat.

RUPERT. I've got to go to work

ALEX. It's Saturday

RUPERT. I have lots to do. I'd like to be in work now.

ALEX. Now.

RUPERT. Yes now.

ALEX. What's now meant to mean?

RUPERT. Just leave the folder, I'll bin it.

ALEX. No, I'll do it.

RUPERT. Okay Alex, I'm going.

ALEX. Go.

Beat.

RUPERT. Why were you looking in my bag?

ALEX. I wasn't.

RUPERT. You were, you were. The papers were in my bag, why were you going through my bag?

ALEX. Go to work.

RUPERT. Why go through my things?

ALEX. I was looking for a sock

RUPERT. A sock. Right

ALEX. Teddy's sock. One of his socks. It's missing.

Beat.

I've been folding all his clothes and putting them in his drawers and there is a sock missing from a pair.

Beat.

So I've been looking for it. I thought you might have it.

RUPERT. Why would I have it?

ALEX. Because it's your son's sock.

Beat.

RUPERT. I don't have it

ALEX. No. I know that. You don't have anything.

RUPERT. I'm going to work.

ALEX. I don't want to adopt

RUPERT. Fine

ALEX. Ever

RUPERT. Right

ALEX. I don't want someone else's child.

RUPERT. What do you want? What do you want Alex?

ALEX. I want my baby

RUPERT. Alex.

ALEX. I don't want to adopt.

RUPERT. What about me?

ALEX. What about you?

RUPERT. I might want to.

ALEX. Well I don't want to

RUPERT. Tricky

ALEX. Can you go? Can you just go.

RUPERT. What about what I want?

ALEX. It doesn't matter

RUPERT. What about what I want?

ALEX. I don't care about what you want any more

RUPERT. Fine.

ALEX. You don't even have a sock.

RUPERT. Alex

ALEX. You don't even have his sock

RUPERT. I can't

ALEX. So I don't care about what you want any more.

Scene Fourteen

ALEX *is in the nursery, painting stars on the walls.*

ALEX. I want to cover this room in stars, endless stars. And
nestle your name amongst them.
I want you to be universal Teddy, I want you to be everywhere,
I want you to be in the stars. I want people to look at the sky at
night and see you. Thousands of you. And say, look there's
Teddy. Because everywhere I go, anywhere I am, all I see is
you. I'm scared to go outside and for you not to be there.
Teddy?
I'm tired. I'll stop.
Can you feel that sun? Can you feel the sun on your face my
love?

She lets the sun shine on her face.

Want to know something? When you're pregnant the DNA of
your baby becomes part of your DNA. You are permanently
altered, the baby is always with you. So you haven't gone
anywhere. You're right here.
That sun is so warm Teddy.
I like that, that little dead-baby fact. You don't learn that in an
NCT class. You learn that your nipples will crack, that you'll
always be tired and that your hair might fall out.
God, I wish my nipples would crack.

Scene Fifteen

RUPERT *and* ALEX *are sat side by side, in a therapist's room.*

ALEX. I feel good, I'm keeping busy.

RUPERT. She's decorating

ALEX. Yes

RUPERT. She's painting the nursery.

ALEX. He doesn't like it

RUPERT. I don't mind it

ALEX. He thinks I'm mental.

RUPERT. This is the seventh time she's decorated it.

ALEX. I want to get it right.

RUPERT. I don't think she is coping

ALEX. My baby died

RUPERT. See

ALEX. Of course I'm not coping

    Beat.

RUPERT. She talks to him.

ALEX. I'm right here.

RUPERT. I know.

ALEX. Then talk to me.

RUPERT. Talk to me Alex.

*

ALEX. I don't speak grieving mother very well. Daddy does, he's got top marks, in grieving father and grieving mother.

*

RUPERT. I feel like each day is easier, and that, while I still feel heavy, part of the weight is lifting, it really is. It's like it was

all grey and slowly patches of colour are starting to seep
through, patches of hope I think.

ALEX. Beautiful

RUPERT. Thank you

ALEX. Well learnt.

RUPERT. Pardon?

ALEX. Well recited.

RUPERT. I didn't learn it Alex, that's how I feel. It was our
homework.

ALEX. Homework

RUPERT. Yes, we were told to vocalise our feelings. Did you do it?

Pause.

Did you do the homework?

ALEX. No.

RUPERT. Well.

ALEX. Don't say that

RUPERT. Say what?

ALEX. Don't say 'well' like that.

RUPERT. I didn't say it in any way

ALEX. You did, you said it deliberately, you deliberately said
'well' in that way.

RUPERT. In what way?

ALEX. You know what way?

RUPERT. I don't

ALEX. You do Rupert.

RUPERT. I don't Alex, tell me.

ALEX. In a really fucking passive-aggressive, fucking teacher's
fucking pet irritating little bell-end kind of way. That is how
you said it.

RUPERT….

*

ALEX. Cynthia keeps sending me healing crystals. She writes
long letters on what to do with them, 'Place the moonstone on
your pelvis my darling and gently hum.' She's never
mentioned you, not once. Her and Dad are off to Corfu soon
and Rupert thought it would be a good idea to join them.

*

RUPERT. I booked a holiday

ALEX. With my parents

RUPERT. I thought it would be nice

ALEX. My parents didn't come to the funeral

RUPERT. You take money from them

ALEX. What?

RUPERT. Money, your mum. I mean Cynthia. I know she keeps
giving you money

Beat.

ALEX. I can take whatever fucking money I want from whoever
I fucking want.

RUPERT. Stop swearing. Don't swear in here.

*

ALEX. If I didn't swear so much would you still be here? If I
didn't smoke or drink or if I earned more money would you
still be here? I keep thinking of all the things I should have
done better, if I was better you would still be here? I believe
that. I think that. If I was a good person I'd have you in my
arms my darling.

*

RUPERT. I thought it would make her feel better

ALEX. I'm right here.

RUPERT. I thought it would make you feel better

ALEX. Better?

RUPERT. Yes. I thought it would be good.

ALEX. Good.

RUPERT. Yes.

ALEX. Good.

RUPERT. Yes I thought it would be good for us.

ALEX. Do you know what's bad for us?

RUPERT. Tell me

ALEX. Having a dead baby

RUPERT. Alex

ALEX. I wonder what the opposite to having a dead baby is, like if that's on a scale, and that's ten, as in the worst thing that could ever happen. What do you think the best thing could be?

RUPERT. I don't know

ALEX. You do

RUPERT. I really don't

ALEX. You suggested it

RUPERT. Did I?

ALEX. Yes just now

RUPERT. Okay

ALEX. You suggested going on holiday, it's good not bad therefore the scale is balanced

RUPERT. I don't think going on holiday will do that.

ALEX. You don't think it will make me feel better

RUPERT. Maybe

ALEX. You do or you don't?

RUPERT. Okay no, not really.

ALEX. Then why should I do it, why should I do anything that doesn't make me feel better

RUPERT. Us.

ALEX. What?

RUPERT. Make us better. It's not just you, it's us. It's me and you.

*

ALEX. We had to find a piece of music that reminds us of you. Rupert created a Spotify playlist and asked me to add any ideas. But all I could think of was the *Funeral March*. It gets stuck in my head and Rupert gets really upset because.

*

RUPERT. She sings it all the time.

ALEX. I don't

RUPERT. And if she's not singing it then she plays it full-blast.

ALEX. I like it

RUPERT. You don't like it

ALEX. I do

RUPERT. You like to annoy me

ALEX. I don't

RUPERT. You're doing it all deliberately to hurt me.

ALEX. Hurt you?

RUPERT. Yes.

ALEX. Why would I want to hurt you?

RUPERT. I don't know Alex

ALEX. You do.

RUPERT. I don't

ALEX. Why would I want to hurt you Rupert?

Pause.

RUPERT. I think we're done, aren't we? I think our hour's up.

*

ALEX. I'm hurting. I think it's from all the painting. I'm painting non-stop Teddy, hours and hours at a time. Up and down up and down with the paintbrush. I'm hurting all over. My back, my arms, my legs, my fingers. But yesterday when I woke I felt a pain in my chest, and I thought: that's odd because you don't use your chest to paint. And then I felt a pain in my elbow Teddy, and in my forearm, then my ear, and my little toe on my left foot. I felt the roots of my hair and I felt a pain, and I realised that I am hurting all over every little bit of me, and it's not because of all the painting, it's because of you. My body is pain.

Scene Sixteen

ALEX. I've cooked

RUPERT. Cooked?

ALEX. Well I defrosted Barbara's tagine

RUPERT. Congratulations.

ALEX. Would you like some?

RUPERT. Yes

ALEX. Are you starving?

RUPERT. I am

ALEX. It's good I cooked then

RUPERT. Cooked?

ALEX. Warmed some food.

RUPERT. Did you have a good day?

ALEX. We did

Beat.

RUPERT. What did you do?

ALEX. Painted

RUPERT. Yes

ALEX. I'm covering the ceiling with stars

RUPERT. I forgot

ALEX. Do you want to see?

RUPERT. Is it finished?

ALEX. No

RUPERT. Oh

ALEX. It'll be finished soon.

RUPERT. Okay

ALEX. Look at it

RUPERT. When it's finished.

   Beat.

ALEX. Shall we eat?

RUPERT. Is it ready?

ALEX. It is

RUPERT. Let's eat chef.

   Beat.

   Ah Barbara's famous tagine

ALEX. Good old Barbara

RUPERT. Do you think she went to Morocco once and now all she cooks is tagine?

ALEX. Or maybe she fell in love with a Moroccan man and he rejected her?

RUPERT. And now all she cooks

ALEX. Is the food of her lover.

RUPERT. How many more do we have?

ALEX. This is the last one.

RUPERT. Thank God.

ALEX. What does she smell of, she has that smell doesn't she?

RUPERT. It's not unpleasant?

ALEX. It's not pleasant.

RUPERT. It's like

ALEX. Cheese

RUPERT. Yes

ALEX. Cheesy

RUPERT. But a very mild cheese.

ALEX. Cheesy Cheddars

RUPERT. That's it

ALEX. Cheesy bloody Cheddars.

Beat.

RUPERT. This is nice

ALEX. What?

RUPERT. Deciding something with you

Beat.

Alex.

ALEX. Do you want salad?

RUPERT. Oh

ALEX. I think I can rustle up a salad.

RUPERT. I don't need a salad

ALEX. I'd like some greens

RUPERT. Okay

ALEX. We don't eat enough greens

RUPERT. I know

ALEX. We've never eaten enough greens

RUPERT. We've always tried

ALEX. I think we should eat more

RUPERT. Okay

ALEX. We need to be a lot healthier.

RUPERT. Okay

ALEX. Perhaps we should join the gym again?

RUPERT. Yes

ALEX. Do more exercise

RUPERT. Get my six-pack back

ALEX. You've never had a six-pack

RUPERT. I have

ALEX. No, you haven't

RUPERT. When we first met I had one

ALEX. I don't think you did

RUPERT. I had a faint one

ALEX. I don't really remember a six-pack.

RUPERT. I definitely had some definition.

ALEX. Where?

RUPERT. My pecs, my pecs have always been very defined

ALEX. Really?

RUPERT. Yes! You remember don't you?

ALEX. You have large nipples

RUPERT. I don't

ALEX. I've always thought you have strangely large nipples

RUPERT. Have you?

ALEX. Almost postpartum nipples

RUPERT. Excuse me

ALEX. Honestly. It's quite disturbing

RUPERT. How are we only having this conversation

ALEX. I've never had a good comparison

RUPERT. I have the nipples of a breastfeeding woman

ALEX. Yes. Lucky you.

RUPERT. How have you coped all this time?

ALEX. Your nipples aren't the reason I fell in love with you

Beat.

RUPERT. Alex...

ALEX. If we eat more greens and exercise we'll feel better. Be better, be more

RUPERT. Healthy

ALEX. Yes

RUPERT. I think this is great

ALEX. You do?

RUPERT. Yes

ALEX. Because if we're healthier

RUPERT. Fitter

ALEX. More alert and alive we'll be ready

RUPERT. We'll be happier

ALEX. And our baby won't die again.

Beat.

RUPERT. Alex

ALEX. Will you hold me?

RUPERT....

ALEX. Just a small part of me, maybe even my finger. Will you just hold my finger.

RUPERT. Okay

ALEX. Thank you.

He holds her finger.

And then maybe, maybe you can hold more.

RUPERT. I can hold your hand

ALEX. Yes

He holds her hand.

RUPERT. Alex?

ALEX. Don't. I don't want you to talk to me.

RUPERT. Okay

ALEX. I want you to hold me.

RUPERT. I have your hand

ALEX. No

RUPERT. Okay, just your finger again?

ALEX. No

RUPERT. Alex?

ALEX. I want you to hold me Rupert

RUPERT. I am Alex.

ALEX. No.

RUPERT. Alex, I don't understand? Shall I just hold your finger?
Or I can hold your fingers, all of them, just them, the fingers?
Would you like that? And just leave your hand, the main part
of your hand.

ALEX. Let's go to bed.

Silence.

RUPERT. Do you want to go to sleep?

ALEX. No

RUPERT. Do you want me to lie down beside you?

Silence.

Do you want me to hold you until you fall asleep?

Silence.

I can stroke your head until / you fall asleep

ALEX. Have sex with me.

RUPERT. But

ALEX. Have sex with me.

RUPERT. But.

ALEX. I want a baby.

Silence.

RUPERT. Alex.

ALEX. Please.

RUPERT. Alex

ALEX. Please

RUPERT. Alex, all I want to do is hold you and hold you and hold you.

ALEX. Please

RUPERT. Ever since, ever since, you've not / let me

ALEX. I want a baby.

Beat.

RUPERT. Alex.

She goes up to him, stands in front of him. She kisses him. He gives in for a second, a small second then pulls away.
Pause.
They stand and look at each other.

ALEX. Please Rupert.

Beat.

RUPERT. We haven't slept in the same room for months.

ALEX. I want another baby

Beat.

RUPERT. You can't just, you can't just decide when these things happen?

She goes back up to him and tries to hold him again. He lets her, then walks away. She follows him. They're close, but not.

You have to... You can't just... Can you give me some space, please can you just back off? Stop it. Stop trying to.

Silence.
She doesn't move.

This isn't how it works. Okay. You always do this, and you never, never, never think of who... Where am I? What am I doing in all this... There is no room or thought. Can you just go. Can you just back off.

Silence.
She still doesn't move.

ALEX. What colour are his eyes?

Beat.

Do you know?

Beat.

Rupert, do you know the colour of our baby's eyes?

RUPERT. No.

ALEX. Why?

RUPERT. Because

ALEX. Because he was dead

RUPERT. Because he was dead and his eyes were closed

ALEX. Yes.

I looked. I looked. I did, I looked. I peeled back his eyelids and looked at his eyes. I saw the colour but I can't remember it, I can't remember the colour of my baby's eyes. Shouldn't that be something I'm allowed to know, something that I should have the right to know. The colour of my baby boy's eyes. But I don't know. I try really hard to remember, it can't be too hard can it? There are only a few options, so I try to remember. Blue or brown or green. It has to be one of those you see. But I can't, I can't. And it's because he was dead, because when you look into the eyes of a dead baby, of your dead baby it's very hard to see any colour. I want to see the colour of our baby's eyes Rupert.

RUPERT. I want to hold you

ALEX. Hold me then

RUPERT. I can't

ALEX. Please

Scene Seventeen

RUPERT. We're late.

ALEX. We're fine

RUPERT. We needed to leave four-and-a-half minutes ago, we're going to be late.

ALEX. Can you grab my coat, the fur one, the fake-fur one?

RUPERT. Got it.

ALEX. Thanks

RUPERT. You don't have to come. Don't come.

ALEX. I want to

RUPERT. But if you don't then just say, Mum won't mind

ALEX. She will, she always minds

RUPERT. She's different now, since meeting Nigel

ALEX. Nigel's coming!

RUPERT. Didn't I mention that?

ALEX. Nasal Nigel?

RUPERT. You don't have to come? We're already late.

ALEX walks in, wearing a maternity dress, she looks different somehow, larger, as if she has stuffed something under her dress.

ALEX. No, I want some fresh air

Beat.

I wonder what he sounds like when he has sex?

RUPERT. Sorry?

ALEX. Nasal Nigel, when he's having sex, I bet he wheezes.

RUPERT. Yeah...

ALEX. Bet he has to have breaks.

RUPERT. Right

ALEX. Time-outs, and half-time oranges.

RUPERT. What's that?

ALEX. Bet your mum loves slicing him oranges

RUPERT. Alex

ALEX. Bet she peels them for him.

RUPERT. Alex

ALEX. Then seductively sucks them

RUPERT. Alex.

ALEX. What?

RUPERT. What are you wearing?

ALEX. A dress.

RUPERT. It's not a dress

ALEX. It is.

RUPERT. Alex

ALEX. Rupert

RUPERT. You're wearing your maternity dress.

ALEX. I know Rupert.

Beat.

RUPERT. Alex what's under the dress?

ALEX. Nothing

RUPERT. Have you put something under your dress?

ALEX. Did you get my coat?

RUPERT. No, I

ALEX. Okay, I'll get it.

She goes to get her coat.

Do you think I'll be too hot?

RUPERT. No, it's cold.

ALEX. I know, but we always get so hot when we walk with your mum.

RUPERT. Take your coat then.

ALEX. She walks so fast.

RUPERT....

ALEX *comes back into the room.*

ALEX. Maybe I'll just take a jumper

RUPERT. Alex what's under your dress?

ALEX. Can you grab the car seat?

RUPERT. The car seat?

ALEX. Yeah, it's in the nursery.

RUPERT. What car seat

ALEX. Teddy's?

Beat.

RUPERT. When did you?

ALEX. I ordered it

RUPERT. Oh.

ALEX. You weren't going to

RUPERT. I would have

ALEX. So I did it. I ordered it

RUPERT. But we don't need it.

Beat.

ALEX. Put it in the car, then we can get going...

RUPERT. We don't need a car seat.

ALEX. We do

RUPERT. Alex

ALEX. Are you going to put it in the car or shall I? We can't leave it here. I will not leave this house without / the car seat.

RUPERT. Alex

ALEX. Can you do it for me please?

RUPERT. We don't need the car seat.

ALEX. I want it with me.

RUPERT. Stop it, please.

ALEX. It's for Teddy.

RUPERT. It's for...

ALEX. Yes?

Beat.

RUPERT. What's under your dress?

ALEX. Please put it in the car

RUPERT. What is under your dress?

ALEX. Rupert

RUPERT. ALEX WHAT IS UNDER YOUR DRESS?!

ALEX. Shout at me. Shout at me, go on Rupert shout at me.

RUPERT. I will, I will, I will shout and shout and shout until I get it into your head how awful you are being. Never ever have I met someone so selfish, so, so, so / ARGHHHH

ALEX. I want to have Teddy's car seat in the car.

RUPERT. TEDDY'S DEAD HE'S DEAD. ALEX. HE'S DEAD, HE'S DEAD, HE'S DEAD. HE'S NOT COMING BACK EVER. HE IS DEAD. TEDDY IS DEAD.

ALEX. That's the first time you've said his name.

RUPERT *walks out.*

RUPERT storms back in fast, determined. He goes straight over to ALEX, he picks her up and he pulls up her dress, a pillow is taped around her stomach and tucked into her tights. She is resisting and shouting, screaming at him but he doesn't stop, he must take it off. And he does eventually. ALEX is a state and sobbing on the floor, clutching the pillow. RUPERT steps back and looks at her, you can see his regret. He goes towards her but she pushes him away, so he goes over to the speaker and puts on some music, loudly so he can't hear her cry, and he starts to dance. He dances hard and fast, and then he looks at ALEX still on the floor.

RUPERT. Dance
    Get up
    And dance
    Alex please
    Dance
    DANCE
    It's good.
    It's so good, I feel AMAZING!!!

He does and picks her up, she lets him and he holds her in his arms and dances with her, slowly she joins in with him and they both dance like fucking crazy, in the middle of the room. When the music ends, they both collapse on the floor, out of breath.

ALEX. If it was a choice between you and Teddy I'd choose Teddy.

RUPERT. I know
    I'd choose you

ALEX. I know.

RUPERT. I love you

ALEX. I know

RUPERT. I love you the most right now.

ALEX. I'm going to break soon.

RUPERT. Let me help you

ALEX. You can't

RUPERT. I can, I can.

ALEX. Do you know what helps me sleep?

Pause.

Just before I fall asleep, I relive the moment I had Teddy, but
instead of him leaving, the whole moment slows down and the
midwife, do you remember the midwife? With the funny
accent? She hands me a gun, I shoot your brains out, you die,
she hands me Teddy, he clings on to my little finger, looks at
me, and I fall asleep.
Do you think that makes me a bad person?

RUPERT. No.

Beat.

No.
I think it makes you a fucking good mum.

Beat.

ALEX. You swore Rupert the Bear

Scene Eighteen

ALEX. When I'm walking around the park, I look for you. I look
at the back of little boys' heads. I look at them and try and get
them to spin around and say 'MUMMY YOU'VE FOUND
ME'. I feel my hand itching, itching for you to put your little
fingers in it and walk home with me.
He is so young and hopeless at the moment. I can't bear to look
at him. He looks like a little boy. Like you, perhaps? I catch
him, eating. Silently. At the table, or on the sofa in front of
some crap and he looks so alone. The other day it was a
chocolate mousse and I thought, what grown man eats
chocolate mousses? What grown man walks into a supermarket
and buys a Rolo chocolate mousse? So specific and irritating. I
watched and I saw him enjoying it and I thought, 'Don't enjoy
that, don't enjoy that child's pudding, nothing is enjoyable any
more.' And he scraped the inside of the chocolate-mousse pot
to really get that last bit, and he licked the lid, licked it like his

life depended on it. And he just looked so fucking desperate and sad as if, as if that slither of chocolate was going to remove all the pain. And for a small second, the smallest most brilliant happiest of seconds it was Rupert, my Rupert.

Beat.

So now I check the fridge each night and if he has treated himself, I go into the sitting room and while he watches the telly and eats his pudding, I stare at him, and each time the second gets a bit longer.

Recently I see you sitting there next to him eating the same pudding in the same way at the same time.
I can see you so clearly. Your legs crossed and you occasionally glance at your daddy, because really that's all that matters. Not the *Six O'Clock News*, or *Panorama* which he makes me sit through regularly. That, that is going over your head, but you're glancing at him, if he takes a mouthful so do you, if he licks the spoon so do you, if he scoffs at what he is watching then so do you. It's so funny. You are so funny. And recently I've seen you and him together in different places, brushing your teeth or putting on your socks, and do you know what? It. It's all getting easier. Even though I don't have you. I have him. You live in him.
So I've stopped looking for you in parks, because you have found us. And I'm going to stop painting this room. I'm going to put down this paintbrush and stop. I am. It's sunny outside Teddy, it's a beautifully crisp morning and I'm going to make us some coffee.

Scene Nineteen

RUPERT. I work in finance
    Is that interesting to you?
    Do you like finance?
    I do.

    I knew you'd leave,
    I always knew

It's what happens
Traditionally speaking
Any human that shares my blood
Leaves

It's 5 a.m. and I have to be up in an hour, I have to work
because the world keeps turning even though you're not here.
This is your room and she's made it perfect for you

So, when it happened
When you died.
I
God
I thought well this is normal, I can do this, I'm good at this

Beat.

I love this hour, this hour before we wake up
There's that smell
First thing in the morning
Breath and farts and sweat
I love that
The indent of the night
The mess of pillows
Her breath is awful in the morning
Always has been
It's like a mixture of garlic and dirt
No, fuck it, I'm being polite, it's a mixture of garlic and
manure
You know that smell in the country
The air around a farm.
That's her breath mixed with garlic
But only in the morning... The rest of the day it's like...
Flowers.
I don't mind
I never have
I love the smell
Shortly after
Shortly after you were... born
I held you.
And I put my face close to yours
I wanted to feel your breath
I wanted to smell your breath

I wanted to tell her you were alive.
He's breathing I wanted to say, you're all wrong.
But you'd left us
So I felt nothing
Just your skin
Your cold cold skin.
I'm sorry
I'm sorry.
You deserve the world you deserve the best, you're the best the bestest boy. I would have given you the world Teddy.
She has, she's filled your room with stars

This is hard.
I'm trying.
Teddy?

Beat.
As RUPERT *speaks, the sun comes up through the window.*

A crisp morning, a seat on the Tube, no queues on the escalator...

ALEX *enters the room, she's got coffee,* RUPERT *gets up to help her. He stumbles and knocks the coffee, she is covered.*

ALEX. Twat.

A Nick Hern Book

Anything Is Possible If You Think About It Hard Enough first published in Great Britain in 2021 as a paperback original by Nick Hern Books Limited, The Glasshouse, 49a Goldhawk Road, London W12 8QP

Anything Is Possible If You Think About It Hard Enough copyright © 2021 Cordelia O'Neill

Cordelia O'Neill has asserted her moral right to be identified as the author of this work

Cover image by Steph Pyne Design stephpyne.com

Designed and typeset by Nick Hern Books, London
Printed in the UK by Mimeo Ltd, Huntingdon, Cambridgeshire PE29 6XX

A CIP catalogue record for this book is available from the British Library

ISBN 978 1 84842 910 9

Woodland
CARBON
www.woodlandcarbon.co.uk
NICK HERN BOOKS
Printed on Carbon Captured paper